Notes from a Derelict Culture

David Solway

Notes from a Derelict Culture

David Solway

Copyright © 2019 Black House Publishing Ltd

All rights reserved. No part of this book may be reproduced in any form by any electronic or mechanical means including photocopying, recording, or information storage and retrieval without permission in writing from the publisher.

ISBN-13: 978-1-912759-26-2

Black House Publishing Ltd
Kemp House
152 City Road
London
United Kingdom
EC1V 2NX

www.blackhousepublishing.com
Email: info@blackhousepublishing.com

Contents

Acknowledgments	5
Preface	9
The Scourge of Multiculturalism	13
Living in the Valley of Shmoon	19
The News from Pluto: A Fable	25
Disabling the Culture	29
Mars Attacks!: An Allegory	35
Shooting the Sheriff: The War on Men Proceeds Apace	41
Al Gore the Poet: Think Again	45
The Pareto Principle: Why Socialism Is Doomed to Fail	51
The Jordan Peterson Phenomenon	57
Confronting the Borg	63
The Problem with Gay Marriage	69
Marxism and Marriage	73
How Smart is Justin Trudeau	79
Feminism's Male Enablers	83
On Scented Minipads	87
A Is Not for Activist	91
Hockey Has Gone South	95
The Unbearable Whiteness of Being	101

Re-Interpreting the Koran	105
The Blue Lobster	111
The Divine Frenzy of Feminism	117
Politics and Music	121
The University Is Ripe for Replacement	127
The Shaping of Our Destiny	131
The Canadian Temper: A Warning to America	135
The Perfect Algorithm	141
The Campus Rape Meme Just Keeps Chugging Along	145
The Map of Love and Misreading	151
Gnostics of Our Time	155
An Interview with	163
The Wild Hunt	169
On Making Love and Having Sex	173
Cowboys and Indians, Canadian Style	177
Is Islam a Religion?	183
The Angel of History	191
The New Puritans	197
Utopia: Good Place or No Place?	201
The Idea of Merit	209
Life in the Biodome	215
The Shemitah	219

Acknowledgments

There are far too many people who have contributed, in one way or another, to the writing of this book to cite every one by name. The list would be interminable. But I would be remiss if I did not mention my wife Janice, whose spousal duties were materially augmented by her research, collaborative and proofing activities; former Chair of the Department of Islamic Studies at McGill University Eric Ormsby, who put his vast knowledge of Islam at my disposal; Ed Dougherty, Robert M. Kennedy Chair, Department of Electrical and Computer Engineering at Texas A&M University for his wide erudition and stimulating correspondence; and Thomas Lifson, editor of *American Thinker*, for his scholarly acumen and for having provided me with a venue to develop and express my ideas. To each, my sincere thanks.

For Janice

wife, best friend, intellectual sidekick.

Meet heaven and earth, and here let all things end,
For earth hath spent the pride of all her fruit,
And heaven consumed his choicest living fire!
— Christopher Marlowe, *Tamburlaine the Great*, II,V,3

Something has gone terribly wrong with our thinking classes.
— Phyllis Chesler, *The Death of Feminism*

Afterward they will get up
all together, and with a sound of chairs scraping
they will face the narrow exit.
— Yehuda Amichai, *Resurrection of the Dead*

The times will be cruel.
— Jean Raspail, *The Camp of the Saints*

Preface

These are essays that both detail and deplore the widespread misprision of our civilization, which I suspect may be undergoing its precipitous denouement as it prepares for terminal breakup. In a time of moral inversion, one might say that a vacuum abhors nature, and the vacuum of the Western intellect in the disintegrating era in which we live will be filled not by facts, by the logic of events, by palpable realities, by common sense or by the obvious nature of things. On the contrary, the spiritual vacancy which has become our home is replete with phantoms and delusions that substitute for the genuine values that have sustained the best part of our civilization.

The intellectual depravity and emotional retardation of the Western elites and their rote-like followers among the masses and special interest groups may have passed the point of no return. In a world in which thousands of people are killed and injured every year in terrorist attacks, in which food prices are rising beyond the means of the world's poor owing in large measure to short-sighted and ineffective biofuel initiatives, in which autocratic nations and torture states are given a free ride in the United Nations, and in which nuclear weapons are proliferating and nuclear technology is coming into the hands of rogue and genocidal regimes—in such a world, European Union parliamentarians hold a minute's silence and blow whistles to honour the seals harvested in the Canadian seal hunt. The world is on the brink of a human catastrophe and what our leaders are saying, in unintentional parody of JFK in Berlin, is: "I am a seal." And blowing whistles!

This is no time to mince words. There is a great emptiness in the Western soul evidenced along the entire cultural spectrum: the refusal to recognize the civilizational threat we are facing, the cognitive deficit and moral desuetude we interpret as intellectual flexibility, the denaturing of language, the absence of political will and, perhaps most revelatory, the faddish belief in the good offices of something called the "international community" to regulate and resolve our most urgent dilemmas.

But the international community is a vaporous conceit. Decisions rendered through presumably transnational bodies, such as the United Nations and the International Court of Justice, are dominated by authoritarian regimes—China, Russia, the Organization of the Islamic Conference and many so-called non-aligned countries, to the detriment of the resolution of local conflicts, let alone "world peace" and the advancement of liberal values. The International Criminal Court, which admits openly despotic states to the bench, is no better.

Another expressive symptom of civilizational decay is the gradual abdication of many Christian and Jewish leaders before the march of another, far more passionate and determined, world-historical faith. The mainstream Christian churches in particular are now in full flight, retreating into a warren of ideological catacombs that have less to do with religion than with the secular and political considerations of the day, their only means of staying "relevant" given the eclipse of genuine belief.

St. Augustine would be mortified could he observe the credal upheaval in which the City of Man gradually replaces the City of God as the locus of spiritual residence (Liberation Theology) or the City of God is still in the planning stage (Process Theology). It is almost as if a kind of ideological alcoholism has taken hold of the Western sensibility. Both popular majorities and intellectual elites blame beleaguered Israel and conservative America for all the world's ills, just as the confirmed alcoholic always has something or someone else to blame for his own dysfunction. But the problem is self-induced, namely, the liberal West's addiction to pervasive self-distrust, the sophistry of neocolonial guilt and the belief in brotherly co-existence with implacable adversaries.

Preface

The truth is that we have grown disingenuous and afraid. We no longer abide merely in what W.H. Auden called a "low dishonest decade" but, far more extensively, in a low dishonest epoch, as "waves of anger and fear/Circulate over the bright/And darkened lands of the earth." Auden's poem is entitled "September 1, 1939." After September 11, 2001, Auden's pronouncement bodes truer than ever: "Mismanagement and grief: We must suffer them all again."

Nevertheless, this is not the time to cater to the accommodationist sensitivities of the politically correct and the wafflers in good standing, those whom Max Weber called "coupon clippers," living off the interest of the intellectual and social capital invested by their betters — religious leaders of conscience, honest intellectuals and genuine artists, impartial historians seeking truth, scientists refusing to be suborned by political and economic inducements, statesman of courage and rectitude. Despite the lack of informed awareness in the popular mind and the corridors of compromising advocacy toward Western civilization's determined enemies, both foreign and domestic, the effort to disinter the realities of the day must not be abandoned.

The Scourge of Multiculturalism

Much has been said and written over the years about the blessings conferred by multiculturalism on the countries that have opened their doors to large numbers of immigrants and refugees. Multiculturalism has, apparently, fostered the (unexplained) virtues of "diversity," repaid a debt incurred by the colonial West to those it has exploited, led to economic productivity and contributed to the putative boon of an anti-border globalist world in which national animosities and military strife will become a thing of the past. This was the idea behind the Schengen policy adopted by the European Union, the Diversity Visa Lottery or "chain migration" program in the U.S., and the hospitality to primarily Muslim immigration in my own country of Canada. Every one of these measures has, by any honest report, proven a failure.

The argument made by immigration and refugee enthusiasts, namely, that the Western democracies were founded and settled by immigrants and therefore should continue to welcome newcomers, is valid only to a point. In the course of time the original settlers created a national identity, a sense of communal membership in a common world unified by custom and law. It is that identity that should be preserved. But owing to many factors, including a loss of confidence in the rectitude and worthiness of what came to be regarded as a racist and imperialist civilization, reasonably coherent societies have been gradually transformed into a mosaic of ethnicities.

My own country is no exception. Canadian immigration presumably operates on a merit system, but there is little evidence of it in practice. True to Liberalist form, our feckless Prime Minister Justin Trudeau is on record as affirming that Canada has no identity. "There is no core identity, no mainstream in Canada," Trudeau told *The New York Times*, proclaiming Canada as "the first post-national state" held together not by a hard-earned tradition but by a shopping list of abstract values—compassion, respect, openness and the like. Trudeau continued: "Countries with a strong national identity — linguistic, religious or cultural — are finding it a challenge to effectively integrate people from different backgrounds." This is true if one sees one's country as a permanent airport terminal or a teeming bazaar, as Trudeau apparently does, viewing Canada as a country defined not by our history or proto-European origins, but by a "pan-cultural heritage".

As Candice Malcolm, author of *Losing True North: Justin Trudeau's Assault on Canadian Citizenship* writes: "He doesn't think there is anything special about Canadian history or traditions. Instead, he suggests Canada is nothing but an intellectual construct and a hodgepodge of various people, from various backgrounds, who just happen to live side by side in the territory known as Canada. Trudeau seems embarrassed, even ashamed of, our Western culture and values." Shades of Barack Obama. If there is nothing special about Canada's traditions, they will surely be supplanted by immigrant traditions. Ricardo Duschesne writes in *Canada in Decay*, one of the most important books of our day explaining the emergence of the ideology of immigrant multiculturalism across the West, that Canada is an extreme though not unique example of impending ethnocide, "promoting its own replacement by foreigners from other races, religions and cultures." The elites of most Western nations manifest the same lack of loyalty to "[their] ancestors and basic dignified pride." The same form of national self-deprecation we note in Canada is at work in most Western nations today.

If we accept that the Western democracies are not mere accidental aggregates but nations with a foundational and settled history, we must be wary of admitting new immigrants in great numbers who may have little in common with an already established ethos, especially if they hail from regimes that are alien or hostile to the civics and culture of the host country. Naturally I will be deliberately misunderstood by left-wing ideologues, social justice warriors and the army of bleeding heart liberals who have lost touch with the roots and principles that ground our heritage and for which our ancestors struggled, fought and died. I am not opposed to immigration *per se*, only to ill-advised and special interest agendas that would weaken and adulterate the stable domestic accords arrived at over many generations.

To say "we are a nation of immigrants," then, is immaterial. We are now a nation of citizens. Skilled immigrants, properly screened and taking into account real domestic needs, should be part of the country's future, but not in multiples that threaten to dilute a nation's internal cohesion, not from backward countries whose inhabitants are all too often uneducated, illiterate and functionally unassimilable, and certainly not from parts of the world—in particular, the Islamic world—whose history, culture, theology and politics have ranged it against everything that Western civilization comprises. The plight of European nations like Germany, Sweden, England and France, sinking into a morass of civil unrest, criminal violence and legal subversion, should be an incontrovertible object lesson that multiculturalism is the devil's gift to a forgetful and undeserving people.

The congeries of welfare recipients bankrupting our fiscal resources, inner-city ghettoes of disaffected and belligerent residents, the array of lawfare plaintiffs, the proliferation of de facto censorship procedures—Canadian federal Bill C-16 (gender identity and expression as prohibited grounds of discrimination), Motion 103 (essentially targeting "Islamophobia"), and the various "hate speech' laws—and the consequent erosion of community standards are the poisoned fruit of such unstructured immigration protocols, a scourge prettified under the term "multiculturalism." A trenchant analysis of the damage to national coherence caused by multiculturalism may be found in Salim Mansur's *Delectable Lie*. (Full disclosure: it is a book I vetted and brokered with Mantua Press; interestingly, Duschesne takes exception to Mansur's "small l liberal" views.) Mansur, himself a believing Muslim, deals with the incalculable harm that this ideological movement has done to the security and well-being of Canada—and by extrapolation, to any nation, in particular the U.S., subject to the liberal delusion of universal harmony.

Mansur writes: "[D]espite the lip service proponents of multiculturalism pay to the notion of individual freedom as the founding principle of liberalism, their strident promotion of group-based demands in a liberal democracy has meant diminution of individual rights and freedoms, or abridging them, whenever they are in conflict with collective rights." Ironically, Mansur seems unaware that his own fervently dogmatic brand of "pure" or "original" Islam is at odds with his deposition, but he remains correct in his assessment. The result, he goes on, is that "liberal democracy begins to lose ground [to] an anti-liberal ideology." The new multiethnic society begins to resemble not a politically mature country intent on preserving its freedoms and maintaining the bond of solidarity between state and citizenry but a Coca-Cola commercial. No western country should feel it has to buy the world a Coke. What it ends up buying is civil discord, political disunity, economic insolvency and intermutual ruin. John Lennon's sappy "Imagine" is no substitute for a national anthem.

The media flap over President Trump's vulgar expression concerning third world sewers from which many immigrants are drawn — assuming he actually uttered the remark — is merely another sign that the West, or its elites, have denied their own historical exceptionalism. Why they should demean their own civitas is perhaps obvious. It is, or should be, common knowledge that an ascendant and ever-assertive Left is quite willing to turn Western nations into dumpsters in order to procure immigrant votes and advantageous electoral results. These quislings demand, observes Geoffrey Hunt in *American Thinker*, "that we disembowel Western civilization and instead venerate all non-white, post-colonial cultures," which is nothing less than an "open invitation for failed states to plant their failed cultures and wretchedness here." Indeed, if Western civilization were not endowed with superior attributes, why would it be besieged by foreign claimants for its freedoms, perquisites and shelter? *Why this mass exodus from countries whose cultures are equal to or better than ours?*

There is no shame in cherishing and defending one's "old country" patrimony and the values upon which civic and communal life are founded. This has nothing to do with an antecedent "Eurocentrism" that ostensibly degrades other peoples or with the risible canard of "white supremacy," but with the sense of belonging to, for all its flaws and errors, the greatest civilization ever to appear on earth, a Judeo-Hellenic-Christian civilization that gave us, among innumerable gifts, the Bible, the Ten Commandments, the Greek library, the *magna carta*, the greatest literature on the planet, the concept of individual liberty, scientific and medical advances never before seen, and a technological, commercial and industrial infrastructure that has made life easier for untold millions.

To gamble these goods away on the premise of the relativistic equality of all cultures, the toxic nature of "Whiteness," and the need to "diversify" our institutions and practices is the very height of ignorant folly. As Duchesne sensibly points out, "welcoming the White demographic displacement by other ethnic groups" is a deception and a betrayal by our guilt-ridden and self-hating elites and their credulous votaries. It is a mental disease leading to eventual ethnocide and the forfeiture of the vast store of accomplishments which other peoples and cultures have not scrupled to exploit and from which they have immeasurably benefitted. Such is a kind of parricide, the killing of the Father whose endowments have been ungratefully usurped.

All this got me thinking about Enoch Powell's controversial "rivers of blood" speech (and revised text) in which, as far back as 1968, he warned of the imminent and future perils of unchecked immigration. Borough life for many was becoming unpleasant and problematic. Native Englishmen were being displaced and marginalized in their own homeland. Of course, he was, and still is, viciously smeared by the liberal press as an unreconstructed racist, although he has proven to be correct. At the time Powell was worried mainly about immigration from the West Indies, which was changing traditional neighborhoods into violent ghettoes, whose first and second generation inhabitants were not interested in cultural integration.

I've spoken to people who are horrified by his "apocalyptic" prophecy that the Thames would be flowing with blood. Informed people know that Powell was alluding to a passage from Book VI of Virgil's *Aeneid* in which the Sibyl prophesizes that the "Tiber would flow with blood" as a classical metaphor for the threat of civil dissension. One can guess what Powell would have thought were he still among us and observing the rapid Islamization of the U.K., the spread of Sharia, the Rotherham grooming scandal, the litany of terrorist attacks and the media-and-government led vendetta against his patriot heir, Tommy Robinson. He would not have been surprised that London now boasts a Muslim mayor intent on soft-pedalling jihadist violence, that eight other cities including Birmingham also have Muslim mayors, that Britain is measles'd with over 3000 mosques and 130 Sharia courts, and, as Dr. Harry Fair, Director of the Institute for Strategic and Innovative Technologies reports, that 63% of Muslim men do not work and are reaping free benefits and housing. And, of course, Powell would have received the same or worse treatment as Tommy Robinson did from the FNM (Fake News Media).

Let's scratch the "rivers of blood" metaphor, since not everyone is familiar with the classical context, and supply another, more current and well-known metaphor from a hit movie, *A River Runs Through It*." Let's say instead that the river that runs through it is a turbulent flood of social division and cultural disorder, from which the subsequent clean-up becomes progressively difficult and ultimately impossible. As mentioned, the disintegration of Europe is a warning to us all. The rapidly fading hope is that the clean-up can be managed, as Roger Ebert writes in a review of the film, with "grace, courage and honesty." Grace under current circumstances may be hard to achieve, but courage and honesty are indispensable if we are to avoid or at least mitigate on our own shores the European imbroglio and the fate of a dying continent.

Living in the Valley of Shmoon

Reflecting on our post-Enlightenment condition, I recall the cartoonist Al Capp, creator of the *L'il Abner* comic strip and inventor of a species of roly-poly, pure-minded, eleemosynary critters called shmoos, denizens of the Valley of Shmoon, who were able and willing to transform themselves into chicken dinners and other delectables to satisfy the appetites of the hungry folk around them. Shmoos, unfortunately, do not constitute a finite resource set, but proliferate in such numbers as to undermine the welfare of society, rendering hard work unnecessary and the reality principle obsolete. They are not, strictly speaking, bad, but as one of the comic strip's characters, Ol' Man Mose, warned, they are bad for humanity "because they are so *good*." They recognize no enemies and, even as they are about to be exterminated, offer no resistance.

"All that is necessary for the triumph of evil is that good men do nothing," Edmund Burke is reputed to have said. One recalls, too, C. S. Lewis' remark in *Mere Christianity*: "Of all tyrannies, a tyranny exercised for the good of its victims may be the most oppressive. It would be better to live under robber barons than under omnipotent moral busybodies. The robber baron's cruelty may sometimes sleep… but those who torment us for our own good will torment us without end for they do so with the approval of their own conscience." But the current political and ideological situation has been infernally compounded, for the ideological shmoos of the day seem determined to feed a hungry and insatiable enemy—whether Islam or Socialism representing a pincer movement against the survival of the West. When "good men" actively conspire with those who would undo them, when the missionaries eagerly jump into the bubbling pot, the end is surely in the offing.

According to our contemporary shmoos, those numinous alchemists of self-sacrifice, when it comes to the encroachments of Islam into the polity and culture of the West, we must run down our culture. Thus we extend the hand of supplication to those who would destroy us, to inveigh against the moral cretinism and venality of the West while fumigating our own history. We must enroll our students in Peace Studies programs and teach them the subtleties of the "deep culture" approach, enabling them to see that our "enemies" are only expressing the fundamental traditions and postulates of their cultures, which are generally seen to be benign or at least neutral. It is our own culture which is warped and depraved and therefore a licit object of the rest of the world's hatred. Terrorism is not terrorism but justified vengeance.

Plainly, this is not a good time for sense and substance as the rhetoric of vacancy gusts to windy velocities. Consequently, out of a fear of offending, a hereditary tendency to political appeasement, an attachment to the runic ceremonies of "conflict resolution," apprehension for our personal safety, a profound ignorance of the Islamic scriptures and the consequent refusal to take the true measure of the adversary who schemes our destruction, we have given hostages to fortune and allowed the situation to deteriorate to the point where we can only hope to, let us say, "manage the damage" we can no longer avert.

To complicate matters even further, for many of our intellectuals and scholars, especially those inhabiting the slum Delphi of the modern Humanities Department, one truth is no better and no worse than another. They have ardently embraced the main sociological tradition of our time which discourages the attempt to establish firm ethical classifications and clear hierarchies of truth-values, flattening all value judgments (except their own) to the same level of epicene insignificance. Everything is in play. David Horowitz in *The Professors* quotes history professor Peter Kirstein of Saint Xavier College in Chicago as claiming that teaching is "not a dispassionate, neutral pursuit of 'truth.' It is advocacy and interpretation." Similarly, provost Roberta Matthews of Brooklyn College was quoted in *The New York Sun* (May 9, 2006) saying that "teaching is a political act." The celebrated bell hooks (aka Gloria Watkins) of City College in New

York and author of *Teaching to Transgress: Education as the Practice of Freedom*, among a shelf of such doctrinaire productions, has stated without embarrassment: "My commitment to engaged pedagogy is an expression of political activism." By "engaged pedagogy," she means taking on the United States as a "terrorist regime" and railing against "the imperialist, supremacist, capitalist, patriarchal hunger to show the planet our nation's force."

This attitude has become encyclopedic in its range. But in "problematizing" the concept of truth, hitching the purity of scholarly research and responsible pedagogy to the interests of political advocacy, reducing fact to interpretation and elevating the epistemological relativism of that early postmodernist, Pontius Pilate, to a cultural shibboleth and scholastic precept—after all, "What is truth?"—our professors have disqualified themselves from adopting a strong and honourable moral posture against those whose passionate devotion to their own, unexamined truth gives them a pronounced advantage in a battle to the finish.

The house of Western culture is in serious disarray as its elitist gatekeepers welcome the barbarians into the family while its scholars dilute the notion of truth, using their baccalaureate clout to mislead, occlude, proselytize and suppress or distort the history of Western civilization. An incipient movement in Britain to drop the Crusades and the Holocaust—and even Winston Churchill—from certain highschool curricula is only the most recent instance of this deliberate courting of amnesia. Britain seems to be driving on the left side of the road in more ways than one. The leftist academic elite—not only in Britain—goes so far as to rewrite or reinterpret or omit whatever fragments of the historical record happen to remain in order to conform to an ideological agenda. It is no accident that, even as I write, the Democrat Party in the U.S. has effectively embraced the world's oldest hatred and, as Peggy Noonan indicates in the *Wall Street Journal* (March 7, 2019), is in the process of going full Mao. It is quite clear that the aretalogy of the Left defies even minimal standards of authentication and will not abide the sober truths of history. No less worrisome, the University as an institution with its Sixtiesh "hang a left" orientation is starting to look like Orwell's Ministry of Truth in which empirical reality is subordinated to a political hermeneutic and the principle of universal rights has been usurped by the rites of identity politics.

It is no exaggeration to say that our political elect and contemporary professoriate have come to behave like Jack Nicholson's Joker in the 1989 film *Batman*, trashing the Flugelheim Museum in Gotham City to the sound of raucous transistor music—Flugelheim: "home of wings," which have been thoroughly clipped, as the emblematic avian plunges to earth. Or like the demon Belphegor laying waste to the Louvre in the iconic movies circulated in France. The repository of the past has been vandalized. According to the the 19th century occultist Collin de Plancy's *Dictionnaire Infernal*, Belphegor was Hell's ambassador to France. Similarly, the Joker is the plenipotentiary of the intellectual Left to 21st century Western civilization, busy at the task of erasing or retranscribing memory. The joke is on all of us.

Not everything is a matter of "interpretation," as in our world-irrelevant intellectual climate we have been taught to believe. One must affirm a truth or, at any rate, cradle the notion of truth, however tentatively, however skeptically, however uncomfortably, if one is to provide the groundwork of genuine education and, just as important, if one is to defend one's culture, community, family or, for that matter, one's very integrity. One cannot simply take water and wash one's hands before the multitudes. Obviously, no human being holds a lien on truth but the struggle to approach a *credible verisimilitude* should be unrelenting. The position of our ideological elite, displaying in its high-minded involutions the fear of anything that even resembles an absolute, and subject to the delirium of a concessionary rhetoric, is little more than a theoreticist shambles, insulated in status and helpless before the exigencies of purposeful practice. Taking refuge in equivocation, they have put their very freedom at risk, forgetting the Periclean maxim at the heart of the great Funeral Oration, that "the secret of happiness is freedom and the secret of freedom a brave heart, not idly to stand aside from the enemy's onslaught."

But we know what brickets our majority intellectuals burn to warm themselves: the scorning of custodial responsibility for founding principles, including loyalty to the nation, the responsibility for its defense and borders, the preservation of its cultural liberties (which provide for their security, both cognitive and physical), the distrust of America (which guarantees their freedom), the hatred of Israel (the only true democracy in the Middle East), the rejection of capitalism and free markets (which give them their livelihood), and the great log of universal brotherhood (which burns only on one side and warms the enemy far more than it does them). George Canning had the measure of these sycophants long ago when he wrote: "A steady patriot of the world alone, The friend of every country but his own."

Such is life in the valley of Shmoon.

The News from Pluto: A Fable

It has been determined by the International Astronomical Union that Pluto is no longer a real planet, having been relegated to the status of a *plutoid*, that is, a dwarf planet circling beyond the orbit of Neptune, a mere rock of ice shambling about in the Kuiper Belt.

The planetary demotion does not sit well with the Plutoniacs, who are up in arms over the astronomical slight to their collective dignity. As PNB (Pluto National Broadcaster) reports, protests have erupted across the entire surface of the aggrieved celestial body, with intense flare-ups in Cthulhu Regio, Sputnik Planum, and Meng P'o, and bloody violence in the Brass Knuckles sector. The governing PPP (Planetary Popular Party) has lodged a sharply worded rebuke with the Astronomical Union. The minority SOC (Socialist Orbital Collective) has gone even further, threatening to mobilize the spaceforce to shoot down any passing probes and fly-bys. The Astronomers claim that Pluto does not satisfy all the conditions for inclusion into the planetary family, of which there are three: solar orbit, hydrostatic equilibrium (sufficient mass to acquire a rounded shape), and gravitational dominance (sweeping up or expelling cosmic debris). Pluto, the Union concedes, meets the first two criteria but not the third, for it is swarmed by Kuiper Belt detritus that reduces it to a spatial excrescence.

Plutoniac scientists for their part argue that, as in the Meatloaf song (Plutoniacs are fond of Earth music), two out of three ain't bad. Moreover, they stress, Earth shares its sidereal neighborhood with some 12,000 asteroids and therefore it too fails to meet the third condition for planetary ranking.

The Astronomers counter that this mob of asteroids are negligible interlopers, scarcely to be noticed, whereas Pluto's neighbors in the Kuiper Belt are essentially planetoids, some like Ceres, Eris, Quaoar, Makemake, Orcus and Sedna nearly as large as Pluto itself, which is in any event too small to be classified as a bona fide planet.

The Plutoniacs fire back that Mercury is not that much bigger than Pluto and yet is embraced as part of the family. The Astronomers retort that, aside from the fact that Mercury is precisely twice as large as Pluto, it is also a special case, in close contact with the sun and distinguished by the mysterious precession of the equinoxes, which make it unique and deserving of its prestige. Additionally, if Pluto is to be designated a planet, they point out, others are bound to follow. The taxonomy of the Solar System would soon be overwhelmed by sheer numbers and so lose its unique character, washed out by proletarian sameness. Planetoids will surely bring their moons with them and crowd the denominational habitat with parasitical Dysnomias, Hi'iakas and Weywots, all clamoring for official status and residential benefits. Is all distinction, then, to be erased? Do not the planets that variously contribute mass, presence, beauty, eccentricity and gravitational significance to Solar society merit the prominence they have attained? What, by comparison, does Pluto, a perennial hanger-on, bring to the table?

The Plutoniacs are having none of it, denouncing the Astronomical Union as lackeys of the terrestrial power structure and taking issue with their assumption of privilege. Do the poor, the marginalized and the dispossessed count for nothing in the planetary scheme? Should astronomical considerations, scientific classification and objective facts be permitted to over-ride the legitimate aspirations of the excluded whose rights remain unacknowledged and whose suffering is regarded as of no importance? Why should claimants from the backwaters and slums of the planetary community be regarded as scavengers merely because they have little to recommend them? Should not the society of planets be governed by the spirit of universal parity? Is Pluto not equal in existential value to Earth or, for that matter, Jupiter? Size, influence, material contribution and evident activity are unearned prerogatives, they assert, mere accidents of time and chance. For are not all heavenly bodies the children of the Big Bang?

The News from Pluto: A Fable

Faced with a growing barrage of accusations of Earthism, helioproxism and Plutophobia, the Astronomical Union has been set back on its heels and is presently reconsidering its judgment as, perhaps, hastily and improperly rendered. Some of its members now regard the new definition as internally inconsistent and others have disclosed that only a fraction of the 2,700 scientists who attended the pivotal meeting were present at the vote. Clearly, the process was skewed from the start and the Plutoniacs, who are presumably not devoid of reason and moral principle, have mounted a strong case on their behalf. The day may have arrived to arrange for a more equitable dispensation.

Although the Astronomers themselves have no intention of surrendering their professional pre-eminence and caste advantages, they now seem prepared to accept the vociferous demands of the Plutoniacs and, in fact, to take the issue a step further and turn the Solar System into a celestial haven where all comers—planetoids, comets, asteroidal migrants and fugitive black holes from the more turbulent and desert-like regions of the universe—will be made welcome in the arena of reclassification. Fairness requires reparation and outreach.

Indeed, as some of the conferees have begun to speculate, why stop at mere tabular nomenclature? Why not think boldly and go where no man has gone before? Re-codification is doubtless an appropriate concession, but more is needed. Physical proximity is the only real answer to the claims and grievances of the outriders. Technological advances in Space Engineering may allow for the eventual redistribution of orbits to create a more homogeneous, intimate and compact planetary alignment, with Pluto and its fellow Kuiper Belters and their satellites becoming part of the inner ring. In this way systemic bias and discrimination would become a thing of the past to be replaced by the sentiment and practice of universal enlightenment. One can imagine AW197 trailing or even leading Saturn on its course around the sun and weird, dervish-like Haumea cheek by jowl with Earth. No dwarf planet left behind!

True, under these circumstances the Solar System would look very different and a "new normal" would prevail, the Astronomers admit.

But perhaps this is for the better. All should share equally in the order of things despite the upheavals, the collisions and the suspension of natural law that will likely shatter the framework of the Solar System to smithereens. After all, gravitational havoc, orbital mayhem and ultimate chaos are a small price to pay for cosmic justice.

Disabling the Culture

Anyone who has followed academic issues since the anti-intellectual 1960s knows that the university is in serious trouble, catering to a professoriate that has bought into the travesty of "social justice," a coercive ideology obsessed with "victim groups." The university's ancestral mission of pursuing truth has been replaced by a species of social engineering and leftist indoctrination. At the same time, it views its mandate as establishing a "safe space" for a student clientele that spends far too much of its time and energy "wringing its hands over pronouns, gluten and microaggressions" rather than devoting itself to the rigors of study and the acquisition of honest merit. These impoverished souls have come to be known as "snowflakes," justifiably.

One of the most revealing indicators of the university's failure to consistently produce able-minded graduates is the institutionalizing of disability accommodation through adapted exams and other measures implemented by Student Access Services. The intention was originally a laudable one: to help otherwise capable students with serious or crippling infirmities to further their academic careers with every reasonable chance of success. Like many noble endeavors it soon tumbled victim to the law of unintended consequences.

Within a very short period, disabilities multiplied like rabbits on steroids. A poor memory became a disability, for which students were allowed to bring a "Memory Aid" to exams—once called "cheating." Fear of exams became a disability for which the student could be permitted to write at home. Bipolarity became a disability for which a student could request assignment deferrals and forgiveness for class absences, sometimes amounting to credit received for a course almost never attended. Habitual time-stress became a disability for which extra writing time would be allotted. Students who are unequal to the task of listening to and summarizing lecture material can request a "note-taker" conscripted from the student body—a permit which entails a host of obvious pragmatic and pedagogical perplexities. Scent allergies became a disability, requiring teachers to abjure cologne or provide the student with an unoccupied room. Difficulty with normative procedures became a disability requiring advance course outlines and transcriptions of what are called "alternative format materials." Dyslexia became a disability akin to blindness. A note from a psychologist reporting a student "under my care" can be used to set aside academic criteria and official class deportment.

Almost every conceivable inconvenience that most of us dealt with individually in our day as students has become a disability needing singular accommodation—a sequel glossed over by the typically bland and misleading language of Access documents stressing "academic integrity" and respect for "standards of achievement." The discrepancy between word and act is glaring. A "letter of attestation" provided by the Service acknowledges the teacher's authority; the fact is that her authority is progressively undermined as the student's demands take precedence over the teacher's prerogatives.

To cope with the deluge of disability claimants, university Access services have ballooned since their founding only a decade or so ago. The dozen or so office personnel who labor under an unmanageable load at my wife's university have to produce thousands of adapted exams. The bureaucratic machinery needed to process the epidemic of dysfunction is subject to engine meld. Adjustments in scheduling, teacher availability, the shuffling of classrooms, calls for the provision of exam questions even before a course is over, the furnishing of hardware devices and software programs, and the according of grades for unsubmitted, massively delayed, partially completed or defective work has placed the entire academic project in jeopardy. I estimate on the basis of figures I have privately reviewed that approximately 10 per cent of the student body benefits from special privileges.

The consequences do not stop there. Decent, hard-working

students — in any event, those who remain — see their grades effectively devalued like a currency. Productivity is not rewarded and morale is sabotaged. Responsible teachers (who, incidentally, are not informed of the nature of their students' disabilities or of the specialized equipment and constraints demanded) find that their workloads have increased, that the directives issued are often non-compliable (e.g., my wife has received demands for, among other things, an ergonomic chair in the classroom, an item she cannot procure), and that they are always in peril of falling afoul of a blizzard of mysterious regulations.

The fact is that professors are no longer in charge of their own classrooms. External administrators and government officials make decisions about how they must conduct their teaching and which students they are allowed to fail. In a startling case, Heinz Klatt, a professor at the University of Western Ontario (pretentiously rebadged as Western University) and a personal friend, was prohibited from failing a psychology student whose mental retardation (now called "intellectual disability") prevented her from fulfilling the course requirements. The Faculty Dean changed her F to a B. Who or what really benefits from such accommodation is an open question — not the university's academic reputation, not disciplinary scruple in the classroom or optimal learning for the dwindling residue of achievers, not the organization that may hire the student, and certainly not the student herself who will be unable to prosper in the professional position for which she has sought accreditation.

Most alarmingly, teachers are vulnerable by law to frivolous allegations of misconduct from aggrieved or vindictive students, which may result in a teacher having to face an extramural Social Justice Tribunal with the power to levy significant fines and tarnish or destroy a reputation. My wife has been summoned before the Social Justice Tribunal of Ontario in response to a disability grievance, which on any rational assessment is without foundation. Universities, and the governments which finance and control them, are endowed with the authority to "disable" a person's life on the flimsiest of grounds. Such is the ironic form of disability — the deliberate disabling of those who are not disabled.

The practice of disabling the able—or potentially able—is now a prominent feature of university protocol, pertaining not only to the remnant of honorable professors but, as mentioned, to a generation of students increasingly consumed by progressivist memes and fundamentally non-academic issues, valorizing feeling over thought and sociological canards—the "rape culture" and "white privilege" fantasies chief among these—over actual learning, study and research. Distressingly, we have reached the point where a student can have a teacher punished or fired for a trivial or non-existent offence but a teacher cannot recommend that a student be expelled for breach of academic conduct or violation of a civil code of behavior. Students have begun to control the parietal agenda.

Thus, it is by no means surprising that students at Barnard College are agitating for a transgender woman of color to serve as the institution's next president. Intersectional identity euchres mere qualification, another "disability project" sure to meet with stunning success. Similarly, why affect astonishment that students, with the blessing of the Penn State English Department, have replaced the iconic portrait of Shakespeare with that of the self-described "black, lesbian, mother, warrior, poet" Audre Lorde, who could not tell the difference between a poetical object and a polemical tract? It is no longer a question of actual, imagined or exaggerated disability but of a criterial pathology which favors mediocrity over accomplishment and ideological purity over professional capacity.

Indeed, disability at every level is the name of the game, the incubator for societal collapse. It has spread out of the academy into the culture at large like James Rollins' Sixth Extinction—let's call it a virus based on the arsenic of ignorance and the iron phosphate of impregnable self-indulgence. It is, as I've suggested, not only the overweening solicitude for those who experience, or who claim to experience, one or another disability that has brought the university into disrepute. It is the general weakening of academic standards, the watering down of the curriculum, the profusion of bogus courses, the focus on political indoctrination, the Bowdlerizing of history and the substitution of pedestrian ciphers for true greats that is turning the university into a caricature of its original educational and civilizing purpose. It is an institution no less disabled than many of the students its cossets and graduates.

Think of this when your doctor has to consult an index card to refresh his memory or your accountant suffers a nervous breakdown when confronted by a complicated tax return or your child's grade-school teacher cannot write an intelligible report card or you have to sit through a poetry reading by a poet who never mastered basic grammar or you meet an esteemed Professor of Classical Rhetoric who cannot read Aristotle in the original or your lawyer proves ignorant of legal procedure or the bridge you're driving over starts to sway and groan. These are not fanciful episodes; I can attest to them. And they are multiplying at a shocking rate.

In *Push Back: Reclaiming the American Judeo-Christian Spirit*, Rabbi Aryeh Spiro admonishes us to "push back against an unrelenting and programmed assault by liberal demagogues co-opting our schools and colleges." Regrettably, we "have not fought back nearly enough"—perhaps because we too have been disabled by the propaganda of the Ivy League left and a terminally disreputable media, having ceded both our saving skepticism and moral language to them. We too, historically speaking, have memory issues, and may have grown allergic to hard thinking. We, too, have frittered away our native endowments.

When the university succumbs to the disability prepossession across the board, the culture itself is at risk of intellectual and functional decay. It grows progressively disabled, incapable of dealing with reality, of managing its economic affairs, of recognizing its enemies, of absorbing adversity, and of disambiguating truth from error, fact from fiction and nature from ideology. Unfortunately, there is no superordinate Disability Office to appeal to, from which we can demand or expect the false magnanimity of concessionary privileges—which would, in any case, merely compound the syndrome from which we suffer.

Philosopher Alfred North Whitehead in *The Aims of Education* struggled with the conundrum of effective priority regarding education and culture. Where does change begin, he wondered, with culture or education?—a question he was unable to answer satisfactorily. It is reminiscent of the enigma of whether nature or nurture is the determining factor in human development. Clearly, both elements are differentially in play. But the university, as the feeder institution for the society it ostensibly serves, is a more cohesive locus than the environing atmospherics of culture as a whole and can be addressed with greater analytical precision. One thing is certain. If it cannot return to scholarly health, the cultural malady threatens to become permanent. And the F will remain an F.

Mars Attacks!: An Allegory

The renowned astrophysicist Stephen Hawking, dealing with the subject of possible extraterrestrial life, warns that contact with an alien civilization could spell disaster for the human race. "If aliens ever visit us," he said, "I think the outcome would be much as when Christopher Columbus first landed in America, which didn't turn out very well for the American Indians." *PJ Media* editor Rick Moran concludes an article on this question with a misplaced aspiration: "we can only hope that any intelligent life that becomes aware of us will share at least some of the values and morals our species holds dear." *Pace* Moran, but I wonder about these "values and morals" in so intrinsically competitive and violent a species as ours and shudder to think that a highly evolved extraterrestrial race of beings may share them with us.

The situation of late, however, is somewhat different in the West, where a certain "transvaluation" has occurred. The "values and morals" increasingly prevalent among us are those of "moral equivalence," pacifism, diffidence, "compassion," self-abasement and pride masking as false humility. In the current context, such ostensible virtues turn out to be vices, which we would be foolish to expect a maniple of alien intruders to share with us. It would be more prudent to anticipate the opposite.

But prudence is not our strong point. The Active SETI (Active Search for Extra-Terrestrial Intelligence) movement and its offshoots, for example, believe that an alien civilization would be guided by the doctrine of universal altruism, a theory grounded in the assumption that advanced evolution leads inevitably to a "higher" ethical sensibility. Walter Sullivan in his admittedly fascinating book *We Are Not Alone* is convinced of the benefits that would flow via communion with evolutionary prodigies. "Most exciting of all the prospects," he writes, "are the spiritual and philosophical enrichment to be gained by such exchanges." Of course, there is no evidence that such would be the case, especially if we extrapolate from our own behavior. It's a good bet our visitors from space won't look or act anything like the diaphanous exotics in *Encounters of the Third Kind* or the sylvan Na'vi in *Avatar*. Astrobiology does not assure moral enlightenment.

But the prospect of alien hostility is not the only factor to be considered. There is the possibility of a fundamental misunderstanding between two species that have no common language with which to bridge the intergalactic gap that separates them and that would allow for differences in thought and intention to be worked out. Complicating this scenario is the potentially misguided conviction that, were our visitors aggressive by nature, overtures of peace and compatibility would be sufficient to bring about a harmonious resolution to the threat of conflict.

Consider the 1996 film *Mars Attacks!* which rather uncannily introduces a shot of the World Trade Center, traces a misguided official policy of appeasement and "cultural understanding," dwells on the dove-releasing antics of the peace constituency which provoke immediate slaughter, and concludes in near-universal catastrophe. These cartoonish little aliens sliding down their saucer ramps proceed to take advantage of our deeply held belief in multicultural accommodation, responding favorably to our gestures of inclusion and shedding tears of sentimental fellow-feeling, only to insinuate themselves into our trust and play upon our fantasy of an ideal kinship. Before we know it things start blowing up and people are mowed down in the streets. Eventually, the president of the United States (played brilliantly by a smarmily innocuous Jack Nicholson), who adopts an agenda of reaching out to our enemies, is murdered in the White House by a gum-chewing Martian disguised as a hooker.

The allegory is unmistakable. The film—to some extent like the television remake of *V* about an interstellar civilization promising peace but harboring ominous designs—is a prescient cinematic transposition of what is now our nineleven world. Believing in the good intentions of our "otherworldly" visitors, permitting a belligerent minority to integrate into the structure of society and to establish organizations devoted to furthering their ulterior aims, and exonerating irruptions of culture-specific mayhem—suicide attacks, shootings, honor killings—as owing to other and even justifiable causes, we have embraced the Martians in our midst. That is, we have given *carte blanche* to the *mustashhidin* and their local variants—insurgents, "martyrs," spokesmen for the Muslim Brotherhood, clever proselytizers, and advocates of Shari'a law—who would infiltrate and undermine the very institutions that guarantee our freedoms.

And they have powerful accomplices. The America-hating Left in the universities, the legacy media and even the Democrat party have become Islamofascism's most valuable ally, a fifth column of *de facto* jihadists in everything but name as it prosecutes the war against Western civilization. Abetted by the profound naivety of a public ignorant of history and educated in the dogmas of postmodern relativity—all cultures are equal and must be understood on their own terms, one "truth" is as good as another, universal human rights are only an expression of Western particularism, etc—the Left, with open arms and closed minds, has welcomed the Martians who would destroy us. Only, these Martians are not harbingers of an advanced civilization blessed with sidereal intelligence but are rooted in the norms and usages of a pre-Medieval world view, which we regard as equally exotic.

How have we permitted this to happen? Have we absorbed our social and political conjectures at so impressionable and formative a stage in our cognitive development, as students in the revolutionary Sixties and Seventies, that we now act from rote behavior rather than critical reflection, bearing witness to the truth of Yogi Berra's apothegm, "There are some people who, if they don't know already, you can't tell 'em." Is Victor Davis Hanson right when he declares that "our present generation is on the brink of moral insanity," victims of lazy thinking, unable to distinguish between the terrorist and his quarry, and subject to the clichés "of postmodernism, cultural relativism, utopian pacifism, and moral equivalence"? Or are we merely hoping for clemency from an indebted foe who will, presumably, spare us for our collusion? Do we live in such a state of inward fear and paralysis that, to paraphrase poet Neil Powell, we are unable to let "panic subside to knowledge"?

But perhaps the fact is that years of cosseted, entitlement-friendly living, not to mention enrolment in the postmodern academy, have made us soft, prone to theoretical delusions, intellectually puerile, and unwilling to face the reality of struggle and conflict so many of us have been happily spared. We appear to suffer from a condition that Robert Wilson has called, in his book of that title, "the ignorance of blood," which has blinded us to the baleful motives of our adversaries. Confronted with a dedicated enemy intent on conquest, we respond with platitudes like "social justice," "equal status," "sensitivity," "diversity," "peaceful coexistence" and all the rest of the ideological claptrap we have had dinned into us. Returning fire with ice cream scoops is no way to win a war. These notions would be fine if two criteria were satisfied, namely, that we were proud defenders of our own storied culture, and that the recipients of our generosity were willing to reciprocate. But when these two conditions are not met, then it is clear that we are not only inviting guests into our home. We are also inviting disaster.

The invaders we have to contend with, of course, are not lizards disguised as humans or megacephalic dwarves toting ray guns, contact with whom we might have preferred to avoid. They are, rather, a group of *intraplanetary* visitors who have emigrated to our shores with the purpose of social inversion and political subversion. Lest I be misunderstood, I am not referring to those who have come to make a better life for themselves and who are eager to join the cultural mainstream, learn the language, familiarize themselves with the history of the nation they have opted to become part of, enter the professions, and live as loyal and productive citizens.

On the contrary. I am referring to what is often called the "radical fringe," which may not be as marginal as we would like to think. Radicals tend to multiply, radicalism to radiate outward. Indeed, we have sufficient evidence by now of sermons preaching sedition and violence, of homicidal rampages, of plots uncovered, and of the exploitation of our legal system and menaces publicly uttered with a view to suppressing informed dissent, principled objections, postings and publications. But instead of fighting back, belling our subversives and deporting their ringleaders, we cower and self-censor, like sanctimonious proctors silencing the unruly who oppose the drift toward supplication, and so enforcing the discipline of surrender. We have, in effect, been ghettoized inside our own trembling world, as if the country we live in could be renamed South Park, no longer the feisty and irreverent place it once was. So much for courage and independence.

Observed through the lens of history, this growing brigade of interlopers represents not merely a demographic trend but the forward cohort of an expeditionary force, taking cover beneath the mantle of its peaceable compatriots. "The vast majority of Muslim legal immigrants," *writes* former congressman Virgil Goode, "do not support terrorism, but their large numbers allow terrorists to blend into the immigrant community." They are the sea in which the sharks swim. Our refusal to act decisively against so insidious a threat to our way of life, by putting the brakes on *excessive or undifferentiated* immigration and by targeting extremists through the agencies at our disposal, is tantamount to gross capitulation.

Returning to the film, we note that the Martian invaders are ultimately routed. But they are not killed with kindness or disarmed by assimilation. It takes a blast of good old traditional American country music, which the aliens are unable to absorb and which reduces them to quivering heaps of head-exploding gelatin, to do the job. We recall, too, that the major theorist of the Muslim Brotherhood, Sayyid Qutb, as he recounts in *Milestones*, couldn't tolerate the innocent waltz music or cheerful jitterbugging at American church dances, which pretty well drove him mad. The lesson the film teaches is obvious. It is not simply the heartland music as such that defeats the "aliens" but *the attitudes, codes, mores, standards, originality and self-confidence which the music enshrines*. It takes a belief in ourselves, our culture and our history, and a commitment to celebrate who we are (or were), to resist the sinister blandishments of the Martians among us.

Failing that, we will find ourselves soon enough facing a very different kind of music.

Shooting the Sheriff: The War on Men Proceeds Apace

Sometimes one is tempted to shoot the sheriff. When we take note of what is going on in the town—the moral degeneracy of its affairs, the raging puritanism that has installed itself as a twisted form of prurience, cruel punishment for perceived sexual misconduct and natural behavior meted out under cover of the law, and indeed, the wielding of the law as an instrument of repression—the sheriff can no longer be respected or obeyed. Defiance of an entrenched administration that wears the badge of cultural authority and determines the politics and mores of our lives becomes a duty.

What I call "the town" is simply the place where we now live, the decaying precincts of Western civilization. In the name of "social justice" and a sterile version of sexual propriety—code for a species of depravity—a once-vigorous culture has proceeded to devitalize itself. Normative male heterosexuality is under assault while gays, lesbians and transgenders are routinely celebrated and are seldom if ever the object of police investigations or criminal proceedings for rape, assault or molestation.

The same exemption applies to heterosexual women who are almost always deemed innocent in sexual misadventures while men are almost inevitably found guilty. Moreover, women who have lied by misrepresentation or salient omission in rape or assault cases are rarely sentenced for perjury or legal mischief. The docket is remorselessly slanted against the male defendant. Just ask the Canadian public broadcaster's Jian Ghomeshi, the Duke lacrosse team, Columbia University's Paul Nungesser falsely accused by "mattress girl" Emma

Sulkowicz (who has not only remained unpunished but received a "Woman of Courage" Award from the National Organization of Women), the targeted fraternity at the University of Virginia in the Rolling Stone scandal, the as yet unidentified man falsely accused by the RCMP and a provincial judiciary of assaulting his autistic, non-verbal daughter (a suit based on a largely discredited therapeutic technique called "facilitated communication," the Ottawa University hockey team (in which two players were charged with sexual assault—and after more than four years of anxiety found not guilty—and the entire team suspended by former Liberal Justice Minister and university president Alan Rock), and Brock Turner at Stanford (the object of a judicial lynching in a highly ambiguous case), among innumerable others.

The feminist attack on a nebulous entity called the "patriarchy" asserting its putatively illegitimate sexist power over the female half of humanity is a paranoiac absurdity, a pathological misandry masking as a cultural verity. The feverish fixation on male sexual "perversion" and on the need for "liberating" alternatives can only lead to social confusion and mental derangement. As C.S. Lewis wrote in *The Abolition of Man*, "There has never been, and never will be, a radically new judgement of value in the history of the world," a truth rejected by the sexual vigilantes of the day pushing a distorted system of sexual values—really a system of anti-values—at the cost of cultural sanity.

Under this new sexual dispensation, heterosexual masculinity is singled out as a pernicious form best rejected altogether or at least radically overhauled, pacified, and feminized. The entire dynamic of heterosexual courtship and mating—its patterns of pursuit and retreat, of display and admiration, of provocation and conquest—has now been deemed by feminist opinion-makers a manifestation of misogyny to be replaced by new sexual identities and configurations.

This "alternate morality," Lewis continues, is "arbitrarily wrenched from [its] context in the whole and then swollen to madness." It is thus no surprise that the juridical status of bestiality has come to the fore as a burning sexual question. The wiredrawn distinction between man-animal penetration and touching or fondling with sexual intent is a subject which has recently exercised the judgment of Canada's Supreme Court. When nine robed dignitaries devote their attention to the intricacies of human/animal intercourse, with a view to distinguishing the licit from the illicit, we know we are in deep trouble. But it is men, male sexuality and hypothetical venereal chauvinism that remain the primary sphere of interest galvanizing the feminist and "social justice" constituency. In an important column, journalist Cathy Young analyzes the new legalistic concept of "affirmative consent" that, were it adopted in law, could turn "nearly every sexually active person — especially if male — into a sex offender awaiting detection." The lawyers promoting affirmative consent "state that the 'default position' should be to err on the side of protecting individuals from sexual coercion. However well-intentioned, this is an open invitation for any regretted sexual encounter to be reinterpreted as assault." The ideological zealots have been given *carte blanche* and the hunt to incriminate men on any sexual pretext, however ephemeral or disputable, is now ubiquitous. This is merely the coital version of what Jonathan Haidt and Greg Lukianoff in a much-circulated essay for *The Atlantic* called "vindictive protectiveness." The authors examined the disaster of coddling students — "snowflakes" — in the university; the coddling of women at the expense of manly pride and domestic harmony is equally, if not more, catastrophic.

"Creating gaping fissures between men and women," writes Bruce Walker in *American Thinker*, "suits the interests of womenists" — Alice Walker's term — as they seek to destroy "[h]appy marriages, joyful parenthood, and peace between the sexes." When male sexuality is persecuted while as we have seen everywhere around us marginal or heteroclite forms that are inherently barren are lauded and protected, cultural degeneracy must assuredly set in. For a culture that criminalizes men and consecrates nonpuerperal deviance cannot hope to replenish itself. The war against men, waged by a dystopian sept of resentful neocrats, means that marriage, reproduction, technical innovation, scientific creativity and the hard labor of material maintenance on which civilization depends have all been radically compromised as the sexual dynamic is fatally weakened, masculinity defamed, and both tradition and biology cast to the winds.

We now find ourselves living in a romcom gone sour. We have reached a point where the sexual bond must conform to a theoretical model that exists nowhere but in the minds of people disassociated from reality. Something like the Thomas theorem is at work here, namely, situations defined as real, though they may not be true or valid, are real in their results. Fantasy can produce malign effects. And the social consequences are conspicuously observable as men grow increasingly wary of women and women grow increasingly unfulfilled in their natures, a development addressed by Helen Smith in *Men on Strike*, Suzanne Venker and Phyllis Schlafly in *The Flipside of Feminism*, and, to a lesser extent, Valerie Burton in *Happy Women Live Better*. Women have taken over the citadel; men are gaming in their parents' basements. As a May 24, 2016 Pew Research Center poll treating of demographic shifts puts it, "Share living with a spouse or partner continues to fall"; the "decline of romantic coupling" and the "retreat of marriage," culminating in the safe haven of the parental dwelling for male adults between the ages of 18 and 34, are social trends that shows no sign of diminishing. The stats are alarming. Reciprocal estrangement of the sexes is nothing less than a social and cultural tragedy—a tragedy regarded by a praesidium of legislators, magistrates, media figures, academics and intellectuals as a collective triumph.

"If we are to be a truly healthy democracy," writes author and motivational speaker Swayne O'Pie in *Exposing Feminism*, "we must exorcise the cultural and political taboo that prevents our questioning and challenging Feminism's issues and Ideology." Our cultural leadership, however, is hopelessly corrupt and patience with its malfeasance is neither a virtue nor an option. The natural order must be restored and a right relation between the sexes re-affirmed. We can no longer accept, from fear or timidity or indifference, a custodial authority that has poisoned the wells of normality. "Men seem to be so cowed that they can't fight back," said former feminist and author of *The Golden Notebook* Doris Lessing, "and it is time they did." Lessing is half-right. It's time that men—*and women, too*—began to fight back against the sanctioned arbiters of the cultural moment. It's time, so to speak, to shoot the sheriff.

Al Gore the Poet: Think Again

Al Gore should stay away from poetry. The poor man has absorbed so devastating a pummeling of late that he scarcely needs yet another crippling body blow that could finish him off for good. One must, of course, admire him for the resilience he has shown up to now, despite the damning revelations that have brought most of his "global warming" work into terminal disrepute. Nevertheless, he soldiers on, publishing yet another book, the ambitiously titled *Our Choice: A Plan to Solve the Climate Crisis*, which appeared in November 2009, and in which he does his utmost to salvage both the earth and his respectability.

As it happens, the earth and Gore's *true* reputation stand in inverse relation to one another, the former actually doing reasonably well, the latter in shreds. Though one would never know this from the MSM where — with a couple of exceptions — we discover that the earth is wobbling toward its doom while Gore strides forth undaunted to complete his redemptive mission. But then, the MSM are also on their last legs, whistling *Kumbaya* as they totter past the graveyard, so perhaps we should take their depositions with a grain of salt, if not the whole salt shaker.

To return to my subject. There are two insults one must be wary of giving when speaking to or of another, for their effect is particularly injurious. One is to assert that a person has no sense of humor and the other to suggest that a person has no poetic talent. Nevertheless, there are times when honesty must trump discretion, and this is one of them. The plain fact is, Gore is a bore. He fails on both counts.

I have never heard him crack a joke and never read anything by him in any way distinguished by wit, verve, levity or even a hint of paranomasia. He is deadly earnest and his pomposity knows no bounds. In his defense, one might object that he is dealing with issues of such forbidding gravity that no margin remains for playfulness or creative vivacity. Yet even the gloomiest philosopher of all time, Arthur Schopenhauer, who saw human existence as a rupture in the harmony of the universe, acknowledged in his *The Wisdom of Life* the importance of laughter and gaiety.

No less damaging to Gore's prestige is his pretension as a poet. It is surely no sin for a talentless amateur to set about writing poetry, but it is undeniably a transgression of the first magnitude should he seek to publish it. For it is not only a disclosure of personal foolishness which an individual may not survive — not much harm there — but it brings the noble craft of poetry down from Mount Olympus into the drains and sewers of the age, infecting the public sensibility, deluding the naïve, contaminating the respect for tradition and high culture that should animate the life of a people, and reducing by contagion the faculty of aesthetic taste and judgment in all the fields of artistic endeavor. OK, so I'm going over the top, but I'm apprehensive that the gods might not forgive the would-be poet for so grievous a trespass. One can just see a distraught Erato, the Muse of lyric poetry, squirming on her pedestal.

I hope it will be understood that I am not engaging in what David Denby in his new book calls *snarking*, a term popularly derived from Lewis Carroll but repositioned to mean the practice of gratuitous malice. I focus on the poem because it is symptomatic in little of Gore's encompassing delinquencies, a textual microcosm that merits examination. It is what the French call a *mise-en-abîme*, an inset or miniature of the larger picture. But the poem also interests me because poetry is a serious matter, especially in an age which has lost its memory of the lyric afflatus. Thus, to adapt W.H. Auden writing on the death of W.B. Yeats, we might say that November 3, 2009 was a "a dark cold day," indeed, a black day for the spirit of poetry which looks increasingly like it may have joined Yeats in the grave. For on that day Gore released *Our Choice*, which featured the poem in question:

Al Gore the Poet: Think Again

One thin September soon
A floating continent disappears
In midnight sun

Vapors rise as
Fever settles on an acid sea
Neptune's bones dissolve

Snow glides from the mountain
Ice fathers floods for a season
A hard rain comes quickly

Then dirt is parched
Kindling is placed in the forest
For the lightning's celebration

Unknown creatures
Take their leave, unmourned
Horsemen ready their stirrups

Passion seeks heroes and friends
The bell of the city
On the hill is rung

The shepherd cries
The hour of choosing has arrived
Here are your tools

True, I have read worse poems than "One thin September," but not all that many. It is a dull, anaphoric litany riddled with malapropisms and marred by an unabashed tendency to pure bathos—no different from his prose. Close assessment of the piece might offer a corrective to those who continue to venerate its author.

Perhaps I missed something in my laborious journey through the book, but why "September"? A literary reference to Yeats' great poem, "September 1913," commemorating those daring revolutionaries with "little time…to pray/For whom the hangman's rope was spun"? That might make some sense, but somehow I doubt it's what Gore had in mind. As for snow that "glides," this intimates something far different from disaster; rather it reminds me of Fred Astaire gliding over the ballroom floor, merry and festive. Wrong word. Perhaps "slides" or "melts" is what he intended. And Gore certainly is not preoccupied with floods "for a season"; there have always been seasonal floods in many parts of the world without portending a global cataclysm.

The rest of the poem compounds the fiasco. A "hard rain," as everybody knows, is Bob Dylan's coinage and refers to nuclear fallout; the phrase is now a cliché. Coming right after the drench of a hard rain, "dirt" could hardly be "parched"; one would expect rivulets of muck and ooze. Why is "kindling placed in the forest" when the forest *is* kindling? And why should lightning *celebrate* the destruction of the natural world when it is part of the natural world? Or is it jubilating over our extinction? Whatever. Wrong word again. The creatures who "take their leave" are clearly not "unmourned"; Gore and his multitudinous acolytes have been mourning them interminably for years.

Another slight but irritating point. I will be chided as a stickler here, but it needs to be emphasized that authentic poetry is always consistent. Let us take a look. This is a poem conspicuously devoid of punctuation, yet Gore slips in a comma between "leave" and "unmourned." A casual reader will not notice so minute a solecism, but genuine poets know that nothing in a finished poem is accidental. Lack of punctuation is a structural device, meant to imply or promote a specific intention, to establish, perhaps, a kind of hypnotic, repetitive and oracular mood in the reader. It should enter the reading mind seamlessly. In other words, it should not risk calling attention to itself by the inadvertent interpolation of precisely that whose absence is required by the connotative strategy—unless, obviously, it serves a demonstrable purpose in the overall scheme, which in the present context it manifestly does not. This is not nitpicking or over-fastidiousness. This is how the craft works.

To continue. Given Gore's conviction that the *modern, industrial system* is responsible for wreaking havoc on the planet, the "horsemen" who "ready their stirrups" seem better placed in a romantic pastoral or historical vignette, where horsemen have been known to ride their steeds into a lather. Check out Robert Browning's "How They Brought the Good News from Ghent to Aix," where the determined equestrians "spr[i]ng to the stirrup." Properly speaking, Gore's horsemen should be drivers fleeing in their SUVs. "Passion" is an abstraction which poets—good poets—learn to eschew in their apprenticeship; the passion we are meant to feel should inhere either in the writing or in concrete, effective embodiments, or both. The shepherd who cries would be more at home in one of Virgil's eclogues than in a poem treating a contemporary theme—though Mark Hertsgaard in his fawning commentary on the poem (an "accomplished, nuanced piece of writing") in *Vanity Fair* assures us that "it's usually a mistake to read too much literal meaning into a poem." But he then proceeds to ask rhetorically: "Is Gore himself the shepherd?" LOL! In any case, the only real, live shepherds I have met and gotten to know ply their trade on remote Greek islands and couldn't give a hoot about global warming, which they don't believe in anyway.

In effect, what we are observing is a performance so embarrassing as to make one blush in grudging sympathy for the bumbling pseudo-poet.

Regarding the book itself, it is essentially a rehash of Gore's previous work, though it does have a modicum of redeeming value: much of the information concerning industrialization, technology, *some* of the implementation costs and *some* government decisions is unexceptionable and worthy of consideration. And, it must be admitted, the photos are impressive. The problem is that the really salient points that spline his global warming thesis are all contestable and largely refuted, but they get lost in the thickening wads of insecure data, the constant downplaying or dismissal of strong rebuttals and the progressively untenable claims that sandbag his argument. As a result, the book ultimately becomes an exercise in spurious wonkery. Many of its outright lies, clever factoids, subtle inaccuracies, glaring omissions and sheer howlers are spotlighted in Ed Hiserodt's compendious review in *NewAmerican*, which repays consultation.

Fortunately, we do have a choice, which is to toss *Our Choice* into the recycle bin, even if we are $35 out of pocket. The poem itself, however, continues to haunt like a bad dream or a malevolent spook out of *Ghost Whisperers*. Its significance, as I indicated above, is that it is representative of the Gorean mindset: the sentimentality, the pontifical conceit, the indifference to meaningful detail, in short, the dearth of acumen and due diligence.

Gore's solution to the supposed atmospheric crisis and the emitting of pollutants into the sky is simple: "We must sharply reduce what goes up and sharply increase that comes down." Why not start by banning poems that pollute the mind? Otherwise, to quote once more, it would "be too late to stop the process that we have set in motion." On the other hand, in this particular instance there is probably no need to worry. The poem comes down of its own accord.

In sum, "One thin September" is a dreadful piece of unmitigated fustian in every possible respect — tonal, structural, lexical, semantic, metaphorical — and should never have seen the light of print. If anyone ever needed fresh evidence for Al Gore's want of discernment and unstinting self-infatuation, this is it. Those who don't have the time to wade through 400 pages of largely tendentious argument and special pleading may content themselves by reading the poem. It tells them all they need to know. And the irony is unmistakable. For no matter how reluctantly, we owe him a debt of gratitude for this unintended exhibition.

The Pareto Principle: Why Socialism Is Doomed to Fail

In *The Consolation of Philosophy*, the 5th Century Greek scholar and Roman Consul Boethius wrote: "Compare the length of a moment with the period of ten thousand years; the first, however miniscule, does exist as a fraction of a second. But that number of years, or any multiple of it that you may name, cannot even be compared with a limitless extent of time, the reason being that comparisons can be drawn between finite things, but not between finite and infinite."

Boethius' insight into the nature of asymmetrical comparison is perennially valid, whether with respect to philosophical and theological speculation, mathematical equations involving infinities, or ideological aspects of political thought. It explains why communist, anarchist or socialist experiments in the life of peoples and nations are bound to fail, for as Boethius might have said, they do not treat of corresponding finite entities. In other words, these adventures in social perfectibility flow from the refusal to ground a vision of the future in historical and political reality.

In order to achieve the possible, it is necessary to acknowledge the real, that is, the limits set by the actual parameters of historical existence and the natural proclivities of the self. Otherwise we are on the way to creating a dystopian nightmare. One cannot validly compare the imperfect social and political structures of the past and present with a utopian construction that has never come to pass and which exists only in myth, dream and mere desire. No sound conclusion can emerge from such dissonant correlations. To strive, for example, to build a society in which "equality of results" or "outcomes"—what is called "social justice"—is guaranteed can only produce a levelled-down caricature of human struggle and accomplishment. We have seen it happen time and again, and the consequences are never pretty.

The infatuation with "outcomes" in the sense of *compelled* equality persists wherever we may look: significantly in education, where equality of result is enforced—everyone graduates, everyone gets a trophy regardless of input—and especially in "social justice" legislation which ensures that unmotivated non-contributors to civil order, prosperity and disciplined excellence in any field of endeavor are treated as at least equal to and often favored over successful practitioners and genuine achievers.

There is another, perhaps more clinical, way of regarding the issue, known as the Pareto Principle, deriving from the work of Italian econosociologist Vilfredo Pareto. The "equality" or "outcomes" obsession is a noxious delusion. The Pareto Principle specifies a scalene relationship between causes and effects in human endeavor. Also known as the 80/20 Rule, the principle postulates, as a matter of discernible fact, that 80% of a nation's wealth is typically controlled by 20% of the population. It has almost always been so.

Such asymmetry, as Pareto and others have shown, "is a feature of every single system of production that we know of," whether Marxist or Capitalist or anything in between. Disproportion is intrinsic to human life, whether we like it or not. Moreover, the Rule applies not only to economic factors but to distributions inherent in almost all productive human efforts and enterprises. The potential for human achievement is never evenly distributed. Significant success in any creative endeavor is invariably a function of a very small minority of individuals. Although the Rule does not enjoy the status of a Law, it is for the most part reliable. In other words, no matter how we may tamper with distributive sequences, life is simply not fair. People are born with different aptitudes and are exposed to a diverse range of formative experiences, leading to personal "outcomes" that cannot be preordained. At the same time, *the sum of such particulars group into predictable aggregates which are statistically definitive.*

The Pareto Principle: Why Socialism Is Doomed to Fail

Distributions of wealth, as Richard Koch explains in *The 80/20 Principle*, are "*predictably unbalanced*," but the "data relating to things other than wealth or income" can be generalized, as noted, over the broad spectrum of human activities, pursuits and behavior: time-management, distance relations, crime distributions, artistic masterpieces and innumerable other phenomena. 100% of most things amenable to statistical calculation tend to happen, speaking metaphorically, within a 20% radius, including that which we consider best in life. It is thus to our advantage, Koch concludes, to determine and isolate the 20% of time and effort which are most productive; the remaining 80% turns out to be dispensable.

Elaborating on the Rule with a view to furthering proficiency, engineer Joseph Moses Juran, the father of TQM (Total Quality Management), which revolutionized habits of thought in business, manufacturing and engineering, posited his "Rule of the Vital Few" in accounting for the disparity between inputs and outputs. As Koch puts it on his summary of Juran's thesis: "For everyone and every institution, it is possible to obtain much that is of value and avoid what is of negative value" by understanding that evolving systems are nonlinear, that "equilibrium is illusory and fleeting," that minorities are responsible for majority payoffs, and that focusing on the 80% at the expense of the 20% in whatever sphere of human activity will inevitably yield negative consequences.

We are clearly indebted, as Nassim Nicholas Taleb stresses, Pareto-like, in his new book *Skin in the Game: Hidden Asymmetries in Daily Life*, to those who really do have skin in the game, who are "imbued with a sense of pride and honor," who are "endowed with the spirit of risk taking," and who "put their soul into something [without] leaving that stuff to someone else." (Taleb's version of the "minority rule" is even more drastic than Pareto's, reducing the 20% to "3 or 4 percent of the total population.")

This is another way of saying that we must invest in amortizing excellence by acknowledging our benefactors, by focusing on principles inherent in all distributions of effort, expense, and investment, and that success is possible only if we trade in what is actually *there* to work with. You cannot bank on fiat currency, so to speak. And this is no less true of how one allocates one's personal time than it is of all technical, scientific, professional and social projects.

Here is where Boethius and Pareto meet. In the political domain, for example, utopian theory proposes a radical transformation of society purportedly in the interests of the 80% who produce little with respect to innovation, personal risk, entrepreneurial investment of time and resources, scientific breakthroughs and intellectual advancement. And it does so at the expense of the 20% who are the engines of real prosperity, creative accomplishment and the expansion of the frontiers of knowledge. Its *modus operandi* is to compare what has never been observed except in literary fables and theoretical assumptions against the millennia of actual social practice and the gradual success of what Karl Popper in *The Open Society and Its Enemies* called "piecemeal social engineering."

Utopian theory cannot accept that you need an *authentic* elite—the 20% of exceptional endowment who understand that progress must be measured against what is already in place, affording a yardstick for projected transitions to something feasibly better—if the 80% is to be lifted out of a condition of poverty or even abject degradation. (The Pareto calculus, it should be mentioned, has nothing to do with the urban legend of the greedy "one percent." The wealthy already contribute disproportionately in terms of employment and taxes to the social leviathan.)

In short, socialism is doomed to fail because it cannot comprehend that we live within the realm of the finite, as Boethius reminds us, and that excellence is rare, as Pareto and his followers persuasively re-affirm. When the twinned elements of finitude and acumen go unrecognized, mediocrity and failure ensue ineluctably. Individual talent, dedication to one's work in the world in which we actually live, and intelligence in every department of life are qualities that must be preserved and promoted for their human uniqueness as well as the benefit of the many. For the end result of the veneration of purely notional and immaterial constructs together with the collective fetish of forced equality is, as history has repeatedly proven, economic stagnation, human misery and eventual collapse.

In the real world of ability and performance, skill and attainment, the race is always to the swift and Achilles will always outpace the tortoise — Ecclesiastes, Aesop and social egalitarians notwithstanding. For if this were not the case, there would be no race.

The Jordan Peterson Phenomenon

When we had lunch together one afternoon a year or so ago, Canadian psychologist and university professor Jordan Peterson, who has risen to meteoric prominence for his courageous stand against political correctness and legally compelled speech, looked distressingly frail and was on a restricted diet prescribed by his physician. The ordeal the press and the University of Toronto's administration, which had threatened to discipline him for his refusal to accede to legislation forcing the use of invented pronouns, had obviously taken its toll. (Note: Peterson was willing to address individuals by their chosen pronouns, but was not willing to be forced to do so by law.)

Our conversation ranged over the work of Friedrich Nietzsche, C.G. Jung and Fyodor Dostoevsky, Peterson's chief secular resources, as well as the Book of Genesis, the Prophetic literature and the Gospel of John, Peterson's biblical lynchpins. His meditations on these texts have obviously struck a chord with his audience. From Nietzsche's complex web of ideas, he focuses on the notion of critical strength to combat cultural weakness and on the primacy of the individual over the group. From Jung comes the theory of the hero archetype, the feral "shadow" component of the psyche which must be both acknowledged and mastered, and the "animus dominated" feminist on a quest for societal control. He elaborates on the political wisdom of Dostoevsky's novels *The Devils* and *The Brothers Karamazov*, and expands on a favorite quote from *Notes from Underground*, "You can say anything about world history…Except one thing…It cannot be said that world history is reasonable."

From the biblical wellspring he develops the idea of creative vitality transforming darkness into light, reflects on the Prophetic summons to integrity, righteousness and the Kingdom of God—for Peterson the ground of the higher good and the divinity of the soul—and stresses the concept of the Logos, the principle that imposes order on chaos and seeks to make the unreasonable rational, which he identifies with the spirit of masculinity.

Peterson is clearly filling a gaping spiritual vacuum experienced by a vast community, primarily young men, who have been deprived of agency, self-confidence and life-meaning. And he is doing so by re-presenting the insights of his sources to readers and viewers unfamiliar with these magisterial texts and cultural giants—a privation owing in large measure to poor upbringing and an anorexic education. Pajama Boys living in their parents' basement drinking hot chocolate rather than the Castalian water of knowledge, and men young and old who have been infected and oppressed by the feminist preaching of toxic masculinity, are in desperate need of moral revitalization and intellectual supervision.

The Peterson phenomenon, then, testifies to the deep sense of spiritual emptiness in our culture. Confronting the abyss, he argues that nobility is possible despite the recognition that life inescapably involves suffering, evil and death, and contends that male vigor, fortitude and resilience are essential to cultural survival. In a culture obsessed with group rights, Peterson points out that absent its necessary counterpart, individual responsibility, social collapse is inevitable.

Peterson's message is not new to anyone who has read and pondered his sources; yet it is new in the sense that he has performed an act of synthesis for a largely illiterate, politically indoctrinated and under-educated generation. As John Dale Dunn writes in *American Thinker*, Peterson's "great accomplishment is teaching, counseling, and coaching people to urge them to live the good life, the virtuous life…The only way he might be ambushed is [by] being targeting [sic] by the destroyers of the left with their name calling and politics of personal destruction," deploying tactics straight out of Saul Alinsky's *Rules for Radicals*.

And indeed, the leftist/feminist vendetta is following the script. The now famous interview between Peterson and the Channel 4's Cathy Newman, a feminist attack dog, was indeed fascinating, a true gentleman and reflective thinker on one side, on the other a vehement harridan and raving ideologue. Indeed, it was not so much an interview as a planned assault, which did not go as intended. Newman came off as a hectoring bully who insisted on re-interpreting each of Peterson's answers in order to place him in a bad light. She quite literally did not know what she was talking about, was no match for Peterson's wit, intelligence and erudition, and could scarcely follow the intricacies of his reasoning. The attack failed miserably. Channel 4 then played the victim card, placing Newman under protection against bruited threats to her safety in order to portray Peterson as the leader of a dangerous right-wing cult threatening the civil order. One can plainly see how the media hegemon operates, by applying Saul Alinsky's Rule 12: "Pick the target, freeze it, personalize it, and polarize it," and then feigning injury if the strategy fails.

The campaign against Peterson's presence and his message is now in full swing in his own country. Canada's main public affairs magazine *Maclean's* has featured an article (Nov. 17, 2017) titled "Is Jordan Peterson the stupid man's smart person?"—shades of Hillary's deplorables—written by a certain Tabatha Southey. It is a sophomoric rant dripping with smug disingenuousness and fey pro-Marxist rhetoric, accusing Peterson of monetizing his unease and of being a belle of the alt-right. She refers to Peterson as, variously, Jordan Pea-Headerson, Jordan Eggman, Dr. Pettyson, J-man and J. Pete the Beet, of whom "most of what he says is, after fifteen seconds' consideration, completely inane."

But Southey declines to demonstrate that she has given any of his statements even fifteen seconds' consideration. Considering pontifical vulgarities to constitute an argument, "What he's telling you," she proclaims derisively, "is that certain people—most of them women and minorities—are trying to destroy not only our freedom to spite nonbinary university students for kicks, but all of Western civilization and the idea of objective truth itself." But in what sense is gender fluidity an "objective truth"? Moreover, the fact is that influential postmodern leaders such as Jean-Francois Lyotard, Jacques Derrida, Michel Foucault, Richard Rorty and Jean Baudrillard are on record denying that objective or universal truth exists: rather, all is interpretation or a function of communal agreement. Peterson is bang on.

The problem with Southey is by no means unique. It is shared by Peterson detractors in general and even by the editorial board of what presumes to be a serious magazine, namely: an utter lack of taste, the inability to discriminate between superficial one-upmanship and scrupulous analysis, and intellectual vacuousness of the first magnitude.

Similarly, Canada's boutique left-wing journal *The Walrus* ran a defamatory article by University of Toronto professor Ira Wells, under the title "The Professor of Piffle" (Nov. 27, 2017.) The article is a veritable trove of gross incivilities, lies, misrepresentations, slanders, and contradictions, coated in a thick mantle of sanctimoniousness—the hallmark of the neo-Marxist brand of intellectual misbehavior.

We are informed that Peterson—here we go again— is "the intellectual guru of the alt-right" who libels postmodern thinkers for money, as if Mr. Wells wrote his piece libelling Peterson for free. (*The Walrus* pays between $1500-$2000 for longer reviews.) We are given, *inter alia*, some problematic statements about the nature of IQ, postmodern philosophers , artistic values, etc.

As usual, calumnies are offered in place of counter-argument. Referring to Peterson's online conversation with Camille Paglia, Wells writes that "he lamented that men can't exert control over 'crazy women' by physically beating them." Anyone who has watched the interview will see that Wells has twisted Peterson's words, slandering him with an outright decontextualization and intentional misinterpretation. Peterson was making a perfectly legitimate observation that there is a culturally sanctioned inequality between men and women favoring the latter. A woman may strike a man with impunity but a man must not strike a woman if he wishes to avoid social censure and punitive legal action. Peterson is not "lamenting" anything. He is merely stating the plain truth that "men can't control 'crazy women,'" and Paglia, herself a leftwing sympathizer and longtime feminist, chuckled and nodded in evident agreement. Wells then goes on to bash Peterson for "echo[ing] Donald Trump on fake news," unaware that he himself has just faked the news. Most of these anti-Peterson types are patently guilty of precisely the misdemeanors they accuse Peterson of.

Wells mops up the remnants of his carnage by falsifying the position of Lindsay Shepherd, the Wilfrid Laurier University TA who was interrogated by her superiors for bringing to class a five minute clip of Peterson on TV-Ontario's *The Point*. Wells claims that she "suggested we challenge [Peterson's] assumptions, correct his willful misinterpretation of the humanities, and reveal the pseudo-scientific basis of his attitudes." Not so. Shepherd says that she believes in open dialogue across the political spectrum and condemns the "authoritarian leftists [who] are social justice warriors." Her discussion with Peterson on *Louder with Crowder*, in which the two were fundamentally on the same page, leaves no doubt that Wells has played fast and loose with the truth. The practice is truly appalling. Obviously, Wells is the piffler, not Peterson.

Southey and Wells are exemplary types, paid dissemblers representing the two poles of Peterson haters, the literary urchin who thinks she is funny and the Herr Professor who thinks he is clever. Whereas Southey is flippant and embarrassingly puerile, Wells appears on stage wearing onkos and cothurnus, a postmodern highbrow who strives to tower over Peterson and the rest of us poor prols like a tragic actor on the classical Greek stage. Southey and Wells regard themselves as above reproach but in my estimation they are beneath contempt, like the leftist commentariat in general that oscillates between feeble attempts at satire and portentous efforts at scholarship, always in the service of a lie.

More recently (Jan. 31, 2018), *The Globe and Mail*, Canada's so-called "national newspaper," sullied any vestige of impartiality and honor by publishing its own hatchet job, in which reviewer John Semley describes Peterson as an "absurd figure," the possessor of a "faintly flickering intellect," a creature of the alt-right (again!), and a "shameless huckster." Such misrepresentations and put-downs proliferate throughout this dismal text. For example, we are told, once again, that Peterson "bemoans the social taboo against being physically violent with 'crazy women'" when, as we've remarked, he does no such thing. The tenor of such reviews makes it obvious that the reviewers are not being honest but are pursuing a specific agenda, which is nothing other than character assassination. Neo-Marxist vigilantes attacking a modern hero, they are, in effect, literary hit men.

Nobody is claiming that Peterson is without flaws and blemishes. After all, as Hamlet wisely opines, "use every man after his own deserts and who should 'scape whipping?" At times Peterson can seem histrionic, at times he is prone to bursts of emotionalism. His writing style is occasionally more pedestrian than elegant, and his narratives occasionally carry a flavor of the bizarre (see pages 290-294 of his *12 Rules for Life*). Nonetheless, I believe we have to accept that Peterson is an engaging speaker and a genuine thinker, understands biological science, enjoys a profound grasp of the philosophical and theological literature, and has a crucially important message to convey. We should also note, with regard to those who impugn his scientific credibility, that Peterson's "h-index," or citation count in peer-reviewed articles and papers, is through the roof. This metric, which measures both quality and ubiquity, establishes Peterson as a leader in his field.

Peterson concludes his book by wishing his readers "all the best" and hopes "that you can wish the best for others." We wholeheartedly wish the best for Jordan Peterson. As we say in the holy tongue: *refuah sheleimah*. May he prosper and be in good health.

Confronting the Borg

Protests against free speech in the name of free speech have become the political flavor du jour. Although the MSM tends to avoid covering these unseemly episodes, anyone with a computer and the interest to go with it can witness online these totalitarian irruptions at universities, colleges and libraries across the continent—Milo Yiannopoulos at Berkeley, Jordan Peterson at Queen's University, Heather Mac Donald at Claremont-McKenna, Gavin McInnes at De Paul, Charles Murray at Middlebury, and so on ad vomitatum. But one gets a different perspective—obviously more immediate, more appalling—when one is present at these public displays of doctrinaire belligerence and repressive violence so dear to the left. One cannot shake a sense of disbelief and moral shock, at least at first.

Just the other day and not for the first time, I experienced this feeling of helpless rage and moral incredulity when my wife Janice Fiamengo was invited by a newly formed undergraduate group, the University of Ottawa Students for Free Speech, to give a lecture titled "Is the University about the Pursuit of Truth or about Protecting Approved Ideologies" at the Ottawa Public Library. When we arrived, we found the doors blocked by a crowd of Antifa offshoots calling themselves, variously, the Revolutionary Student Movement and Ottawa against Fascism, pre-programmed automatons wearing masks, carrying placards and blaring slogans through bullhorns. One of these slogans was paradoxically apt: No Platform for Hate. No Debate.

A scuffle broke out. We were barred from entering by a phalanx of massed bodies. Janice was slandered as a fascist, a hater and a rape apologist. I got into a shoving match to defend my wife from potential harm. The paid security guards merely backed away. The police finally arrived and eventually cleared the entrances, but did so with kid gloves, patiently explaining to the assembled thugs that they had the right to demonstrate but not to prevent entry—an instance of "soft" or "selective" policing that is now the norm. When I pointed out to the officers that the protesters were in violation of the law—Bill C-309 which makes it a criminal offence to wear masks in public and the Trespass to Property Act which likewise establishes penalties in the Criminal Code for obstructing access to public venues—and that immediate arrest of the lawbreakers was in order, I received a non-committal shrug in response. I should say that I do not blame most of these officers; they are acting under strict orders from higher up.

The saga was not yet over. As we were setting up in the designated auditorium and Janice was preparing her talk, the fire alarm was pulled and we were forced to evacuate the building, which put an end to the proceedings. The false alarm, of course, is a standard tactic of disruption and yet another convictable offence. We have experienced this so often that I've suggested we come equipped with ear plugs.

Another thing that strikes me about these protesting hordes—apart from their proclivity to break the law with customary impunity—is the monumental ignorance they exhibit. The few protesters I have actually managed to talk to over the years have never read the works of the people they are shutting down. Among an abbreviated list: They know absolutely nothing about Paul Nathanson or Cathy Young, whose public lectures they have disrupted. They have not read a word of David Horowitz, who speaks accompanied by bodyguards. They have not consulted Jordan Peterson's *12 Rules for Life* or attended his lectures on Jungian archetypes, Christian theology or English Common Law. They have no familiarity whatsoever with the magisterial oeuvre of Charles Murray. It goes on.

They do not even know their own origins, having never cracked the spine of *Das Kapital* or heard of Antonio Gramsci and "the long march through the institutions," his colleague Goerg Lukacs, or the Frankfurt School kingpins like Theodore Adorno, Max Horkheimer, and Erich Fromm. They are ignorant even of Herbert Marcuse whose theories they are aggressively putting into practice. Like a contemporary, ideologically primed version of the *Star Trek* Borg, they march in lockstep, spout slogans and commit acts of violence, regarding themselves as heroes of the coming Utopia. (Obviously, they have never heard of Thomas More either.) We have seen this commitment to mindless violence in the service of a presumed higher good before in Hitler Youth and Sixties-inspired groups like the Red Brigades in Italy and Baader Meinhoff in Germany.

The current brigades are vastly more ignorant than the latter two groups, who at least knew their sources, but for a sect that doesn't know what it's doing but knows how to do it, they are remarkably adept. Masks and hoodies not only obscure identification but prevent personal contact. Placards are used as door-jammers and sometimes as weapons. Bullhorns prevent dialogue, in other words, No Debate. The term "fascist" endlessly repeated as a slur against speakers is both a misnomer and a misapplication—in other words, a Platform for Hate—since it is the protestors who are employing fascist methods of intimidation and closure.

Their ideology, formulated in Marcuse's seminal 1968 essay, *Repressive Tolerance*—that is, freedom depends upon repressing others, particularly conservatives and free marketers—and in his widely circulated *One-Dimensional Man*, functions as the ground of their actions. Marcuse advocated in the latter for "new modes of realization," by which he meant, inter alia, "freedom...from earning a living"—a thesis recently adopted by Democrat Congresswoman Alexandria Ocasio-Cortez's Green New Deal—a condition perfectly exemplified by the shiftless and materially idle population of militant students and welfare-supported political hoodlums who assault law-abiding citizens, monitor ideas, snuff out open discussion and pull fire alarms. Marcuse, a cynosure of the left, was himself an escapee from fascist Germany, but as Jonah Goldberg points out in *Liberal Fascism*, the same techniques of totalitarian repression are common to both Marxism and fascism.

All this is bad enough, but what is even more alarming is that the

Borg enjoys the support, whether tacit or explicit, of university administrators, a politicized professoriate, a suborned media network and the police establishment whose officers, as I have mentioned, are instructed to tread lightly. Although in this case one protestor was arrested for mischief—a rarity—generally the police will nab those who fight back as if they were the instigators of public disturbances. Thus, the bureaucratic echelon that represents the law effectively breaks the law by refusing to enforce it. Authority is complicit with the violators. The phrase "law enforcement" becomes another misnomer.

And the irony is palpable. As Janice pointed out in a post-event interview and an Ottawa Citizen report, pro-life activists on campus peacefully holding signs and obstructing no one are immediately apprehended and face disciplinary proceedings, for example, at the University of Calgary and Carleton University, among others. It is no stretch to imagine that a group protesting an Islamic colloquy or a feminist conclave would be arrested on the spot and charged with creating a public nuisance. What we are observing is not only selective policing but the selective application of the law.

The hooligans who prevented my wife from delivering her talk numbered maybe two dozen, sufficient to sink an articulate analysis with a barrage of loudly chanted drivel and obloquy—perhaps less distressing than the occasion at the University of Toronto when she was hustled into a police cruiser for her protection. But whether in small or large deployments, the guerillas adopt the same tactics and are motivated by the same ideology. I still have trouble believing what I see, but as they say, seeing is believing. Naturally I need to be particularly sensitive and alert since I cannot allow harm to befall my wife. Jordan Peterson has called her "a tough cookie" but that is no guarantee against libel and physical threat.

In any event, sanctioned anarchy, especially when one experiences it intimately and on a more or less regular basis, serves as a vivid wake-up call. I could wish more people had the dubious opportunity to note first-hand what is happening to their culture. Possibly then something might be done about it. Regrettably, many I have spoken to have no idea of the current state of cultural disarray, the decline of civility, media corruption, academic decadence, authoritarian indifference to democratic principles and the rule of law, and the political subversion practiced by the revolutionary left. They fail to realize that we are in a state of war and that truth, honor and decency are daily casualties. They have never contemplated Pastor Niemöller's premonitory poem. They think the term "progressivism" means "progress."

It is as if our cultural and political leaders, like the elite in Constantine Cafavy's great poem "Waiting for the Barbarians," were eagerly awaiting the barbarians and were bitterly aggrieved when they didn't show. There is no longer any reason for disappointment. Our mandarins have got their wish. Peterson wryly remarked, as swarms of Antifa clones were pounding at the door and breaking windows during his brilliant presentation at Queen's, that "the barbarians are at the gate." In a way, this was not quite accurate. They are here milling among us, inhabiting the universities, marching in the streets, dismantling the civil order, engaged in the perversion of values, and, like Marcuse, promoting tyranny in the name of freedom. Their freedom.

The barbarians are not at the gate. The barbarians are inside the gate.

The Problem with Gay Marriage

Lately I've been thinking of a former close friend and colleague who happens to be one of the most brilliant and insightful political writers of our time. I had referenced his work in my own books long before I got to know him and was honored to find after we'd met that the esteem was mutual. I regarded his camaraderie as one of the blessings that conservative affiliations can afford, especially to those toiling in the scribbling trade.

Our relationship lasted many years. We met often when he visited our shores, enjoyed many pleasant, conversation-rich dinners, shared the same circle of friends, continued to read one another's works with admiration, exchanged emails several times a week, and even wrote for the same magazines. I introduced him to my wife with whom he developed a friendship and appreciation for her own contributions to the conservative movement. We were like an extended family. What could possibly go wrong?

The short answer is: a lot. Our relationship foundered over the vexed issue of gay marriage, for my friend was gay and expected us to affirm the legalization of gay marriage in the United States and his forthcoming betrothal to his longtime partner. And this we could not do. He objected to a rather obscure Facebook comment in which my wife deplored how the gay lobby's justifiable plea for tolerance, with which she was fully on board, had morphed into the triumphalist demand for the unconditional celebration of all things gay, from gay politicking to Gay Pride to gay marriage.

The question of religious freedom and belief, sanctioned by the Constitution, also entered into the equation. She supported the right of a Christian baker to refuse preparing a cake for a gay wedding. And this my friend could not accept. An email arrived accusing us of homophobia and informing us that the friendship was over.

Although I regard the reduction of identity to one's sexual preferences, *whatever these might be*, as a diminishment of the complex spectrum of human personality, I have nothing against the practice of homosexuality — to each his own — and considered it a non-issue and none of my business. I do not like to interfere in other people's personal lives. Then and now, however, I believed as a matter of principle that gay marriage was another kettle entirely. People can manage their private passions as they wish, provided they remain within the common law, but marriage has to be defended not only as a binding compact between two people and/or an expression of religious faith, but as a social institution whose role is twofold: the preservation of cultural life and the procreation of the species.

For these reasons, marriage can only be a contract between a man and woman. Love, companionship, spiritual and intellectual reciprocity are desirable goods, but from the *institutional perspective* such golden qualities are sufficient though not necessary conditions. As the backbone of the social covenant and *the sine qua non* of reproductive duration, marriage is more than merely a ritual performance or a consumer accessory. Romance and compatibility will sweeten and strengthen commitment and avowal, but the essential point is that the contractual heterosexual union is the driving force of human culture and the warranty of human survival.

When the institution of marriage is compromised, when single mothers proliferate and are even applauded, when children are separated or alienated from their parents, when the bonds of heterosexual intimacy are breached, when gender politics sabotage concord between the sexes, when same sex couples receive the same rights, privileges and rewards as child-bearing couples, and when matrimony becomes the prerogative of any group whatsoever with no relation to fecundity or cultural stability, the underpinnings of Western society will inevitably collapse.

This is why Marxism, for example, considers traditional marriage an institution that needs to be destroyed, since procreant marriage with all its attendant responsibilities is the foundation of bourgeois society. This is why its dissolution or misprision is a prerequisite for the revolutionary socialist state in which the pivotal loyalty of the individual belongs to the sovereign collective, not to the family. And this is why gay marriage has been serially championed by the new Left.

Marriage in its orthodox acceptation may be in some respects a flawed institution; nevertheless, it is imperative. It is the basis of civilizational survival, just as the heterosexual union in whatever form it may assume guarantees the survival of the race. Gay marriage, *taken to its reductio ad absurdum*, would terminate in the disappearance of the human race from the face of the earth. In weakening the institution of heterosexual marriage, gay spouses actually endorse the logic of species annihilation.

Moreover, to contend, as gay couples do, that they can adopt children or rely on sperm donors merely accentuates the paradox, for they reveal themselves as dependent on precisely the sexual fertility which they lack and the procreative function they have renounced. There would be no gays in the absence of the bonded heterosexual couple that rears children and is socially constrained to provide for their future. There is a debt to be paid in the only way possible: do not insult or damage the institution that gave you existence and continues to sustain it. The fact often adduced by skeptics that not all heterosexual unions are fertile or permanent is beside the point; the ancestral purpose of marriage as an institution remains intact.

There is another paradox regarding gays who, like my former friend, are politically conservative, since they have participated in the socialist and communist paradigm of family abolition and the destruction of the very society they have taken for granted, espousing as they do a kind of archetypal sterility. They are doing the Left's bidding—professed conservatives eroding the traditional foundation of heteronormative society, turning marriage into a mockery of its reason for being. The cognitive dissonance is startling.

None of these considerations carried any weight with my literary colleague, who accused my wife and I of rejecting his "essential humanity" and broke off all communication, saying the issue was "non-negotiable" and all discussion would henceforth cease. We have never heard from him again. That his sexual proclivities were wholly indifferent to us and that we explicitly wished the best for him and his partner was now immaterial. That he was helping to consummate the cultural mission of the Left simply did not factor.

I think of our lost friendship with regret. We still follow his political writing devoutly, though we miss the conversations and lament the forfeiture of mutual affection. But there's no help for it. My brief, as I've stressed, was never against him or the nature of his desire and love. My argument was, one might say, clinical. The received institution of marriage, whether regarded as sacrosanct or purely functional, is indispensable to both culture and race and should not be enfeebled or caricatured or rendered moot. It has to respected and maintained in order to serve its original purpose.

My friend would have none of it. He demanded total assent and expected our congratulations. But as he once wrote me about another matter, "You don't owe a friend a lie." It's a maxim worth living by.

Marxism and Marriage

In its centuries-long efforts to dismantle the load-bearing structures of traditional and classical liberal society, Marxist dogma in its various forms—Communism, Socialism. Neo-Marxism, Cultural Marxism—has embarked on a sustained campaign to weaken and ultimately to abolish the institution of marriage as it has been commonly understood since time immemorial. The dissolution or misprision of marriage, as a contract between a man and a woman committed to raising a family and recognizing its attendant responsibilities, is a prerequisite for the revolutionary socialist state in which the pivotal loyalty of the individual belongs to the sovereign collective, not to the family.

Advocacy and legislation that sunder the intimate love between a man and a woman, that deprive children of male *and* female parental role models, that compromise the integrity of the family and that dissolve the purpose of marriage as a guarantor of cultural longevity are indispensable strategies essential to realizing the Left's master plan. Dismissing the nuclear family as an archaic and repressive arrangement whose time has passed, the state would then operate *in loco parentis*.

The problem for the Left is that the family is a traditional dynamic that precedes and eclipses the tenure of the authoritarian state, not only because it encourages a prior allegiance but because it allows for the retention of inheritance and property rights within the generational unit. This is anathema to the Marxist vision of, in historian Jacob Talmon's phrase from *The Origins of Totalitarian Democracy*, the "all-property-owning state," a function of "political Messianism." The Marxist offensive against marriage may be seen, in part, as the ideological version of a corporate takeover.

Marx himself married his childhood sweetheart Jenny von Westphalen and remained married to her, although his political views did not consort with his lifelong domesticity. In the *Communist Manifesto* and *The German Ideology*, he defined marriage as legalized prostitution and a form of female slavery. The fact that he was desperately improvident and ignorant of economics, as Mary Gabriel shows in her fascinating study of the man *Love and Capital*, did not prevent him from constructing vast hypotheses grounded neither on his conduct nor his personal experience. Despite his internal contradictions, he was undoubtedly the most instrumental figure in the campaign to demolish the scaffoldings of customary society, including marriage and the family.

Marx's collaborator and patron Friedrich Engels' *The Origin of the Family, Private Property and the State* has made the Left's ultraist agenda absolutely clear, referring to "the pairing family and inoculated monogamy" as a community of "leaden ennui" and a *modus operandi* for the class-and-masculine oriented "bequeathment of property." It had to be smashed.

An effective way to destroy marriage and the family was advanced by Communist theorist Gyòrgy Lukács, who introduced the concept of "cultural terrorism" which involved the liquidation of religion, monogamy and the ostensibly male-dominated family. Lukács advocated the introduction in the schools of—and as a minister in the 1919 Hungarian Bolshevik government of Béla Kun actually installed—courses on free love, sexual liberation and Freud's notion of polymorphous perversity, which he believed a revolutionary necessity.

We see his pernicious influence at work today in the cultural obsession with sex, the zeal for gender re-assignment, and the insensate proliferation of pronominal genders into a Heinz 57 omnium-gatherum. It is also a cardinal value in the education establishment, for example in my home province of Ontario where, under the direction of former Premier Kathleen Wynne, an avowed lesbian, sex-ed classes for young children exposed them to varieties of sexual practices far beyond their level of emotional development.

Marxism and Marriage

Of course, Leftism attempts to dismantle conventional society by unleashing a multi-pronged assault against it, including rewriting history, undermining religious observance and subverting traditional morality, a program sedulously advanced by the pseudo-discipline of "Critical Theory." This pedantic and ostentatious schematism was promoted by clique of salon provocateurs known as the Frankfurt School in their effort to develop what they called "social emancipatory strategies." They were the answer to the rhetorical question Lukács asked in his 1916 study *The Theory of the Novel*: "Who will save us from Western civilization?"

Thus Frankfurt maven Theodore Adorno's influential (co-authored) *The Authoritarian Personality* denounced standard gender roles and sexual mores as "social prejudice," psychological dysfunction and a catalyst for fascism. Popular Frankfurter Herbert Marcuse's *Eros and Civilization* privileged unrestrained sexuality and all forms of gender deviancy over traditional codes of sexual and family propriety. Wilhelm Reich, who is said to have coined the phrase "the sexual revolution," invented the orgone box as an all-purpose therapy machine and radiant "accumulator" to revive and stimulate sexual energy. Other eminent names associated with the School and peddling its ruinous ideology are Max Horkheimer, a Director of the Institute, psychoanalyst Erich Fromm, sociologist Jürgen Habermas and philosopher Agnes Heller. Their combined intellectual power is formidable, but it is totally devoid of wisdom and practical good sense.

Admittedly, we know, as *PJ Media* columnist Sarah Hoyt points out, that "Once in power, every leftist regime is sexually repressive"—but that is for later, after the revolution has succeeded or a national despotism has been established. One may also note the apparent contradiction in Leftist sexual politics which hypes the nonsensical campus rape meme and launches a vendetta against men, especially straight white males, while at the same time teaching grade-schoolers about sexual variations and instructing co-eds in the use of dental dams, latex accessories and sex toys. The contradiction is only apparent since the mandate of the Left is to disrupt the bond between men and women. Men grow reluctant to marry and women increasingly fail to make good wives and mothers. Same sex relationships become more and more common and same sex marriage has been legalized in 26 countries.

The putatively enlightened Eric Anderson, an academic who teaches Sport, Masculinities and Sexualities at the University of Winchester U.K and is a former student of prominent Stony Brook feminist Michael Kimmel, considers this development a manifestation of "inclusive masculinity" and an evolution in cultural sensitivity. He is particularly proud of the supposed "cuddling" phenomenon among male millennials who like kissing men, and has marshalled a salmagundi of dodgy statistics to prove his contestation. Anderson and Kimmel are illustrations of how the erotic fraternity surreptitiously advances its cause under the sign of presumably open-minded sophistication. In the last analysis, these *soi-disant* cultivated visionaries happily serve the Left's agenda.

As noted, the Left has many weapons in its incendiary arsenal, but perhaps its most piercing labret in its war against the traditional family is the penetration of the institution of marriage and its replacement by an indiscriminate caricature of its original purpose. Its advocacy for same sex marriage is therefore not surprising. It is true that Communism may once have purged gays and, as Hoyt implies, will do so again, but in its assault on the family structure its socialist epigones have long jumped on the gay marriage bandwagon. As Paul Kengor writes in *Takedown: From Communists to Progressives, How the Left Has Sabotaged Family and Marriage*, "As long as the traditional family is reversed, Marxism is advanced." Gay marriage, he continues, is "an ideal, handy device to destroy the family." This is precisely what many gays of a conservative persuasion, as the previous chapter stressed, refuse to understand.

Lest I be misunderstood, I do not endorse civil restrictions on or repression of homosexuality. *So long as common law remains in force* (e.g., proscribing pedophilia or polygamy), couples should be free to follow their passions and desires. They are free to enjoy recreational sex or to love whomever they wish. As the late Canadian Prime Minister Pierre

Trudeau famously said, "There's no place for the state in the bedrooms of the nation." But when same sex couples usurp the fiscal, estate and legal privileges of productive and nurturing procreant families — truly an unearned increment — and certainly when the right to marry can be claimed by any category of individuals and any cosplay group with no relation to the traditional armature of Western civilization, the disintegration of social norms and usages must inevitably follow. As Engels and company knew, marriage and the family comprise the ground on which the battle is most auspiciously fought.

Armed with both the theoretical and empirical power of sexual license, the Left now appears unassailable, cresting with self-assurance. Its campaign against the institution of marriage seems close to fulfillment. There can be little doubt that once the traditional institution of marriage, or even binding common law (*sui iuris*) arrangements between heterosexual couples, have been disabled, when forms of sexual deviance are encouraged, when men go MGTOW (Men Going Their Own Way) and women are regarded as victims of the so-called patriarchal family, and when same sex marriage has been ordained and consecrated as normal, the new dialectic of Marxist inversion may well have won the day.

How Smart is Justin Trudeau

Much has been made of Canadian PM Justin Trudeau's recent exploits, avidly devoured by the press and lapped up by his dazzled acolytes. The latest installment in the Trudeau saga involves a photo just circulated of Trudeau balancing on a conference table in the advanced yogic Mayurasana or "peacock" pose, which has sent the media into yet another Trudeau frenzy and his fans swooning with adoration. Take a look:

Justin Trudeau in 'peacock' pose.

One admirer tweets: "This guy is just too good to be true." Another: "I'm so happy to be Canadian." As CBC News puts it: *"Photo of Justin Trudeau doing yoga makes the internet freak out - again."* In my estimation, this is not a posture befitting a head of state - but maybe that's just me.

A few days earlier, media focus was on Trudeau's apparently uncanny brain power, to wit, a "stunning" riff on the topic of quantum computing. The media, of course, failed to report that Trudeau's Wikipedia stunt was set up by Trudeau himself, who asked to be asked so he could reel off a couple of boilerplate lines he had obviously memorized. According to the *Daily Mail*, "*Justin Trudeau stuns room full of reporters and scientists with perfect answer to complex quantum computing question.*" Here is Trudeau's reply to a journalist's stuttering query ("I was going to ask you about quantum computing, but ..."):

> "Very simply, normal computers work by ...', he began before he was interrupted by the crowd's shocked laughter. "No, no, don't interrupt me, when you walk out of here you will know more — well no, some of you will know far less — about quantum computing. Normal computers work by ... either the power going through a wire or not. It's 1 or a 0. They're binary systems. What quantum states allow for is much more complex information to be encoded into a single bit. A regular computer bit is either a 1 or 0 - on or off. A quantum state can be much more complex than that because as we know, things can be both particles and waves at the same time. And the uncertainty around quantum states allows us to encode more information into a much smaller computer."

So far as I can see, the question is neither "complex" nor the answer "perfect." Note how Trudeau says nothing about the real problem, namely quantum indeterminacy and how to manage the superposition of incompatible states reliably and practically. Nor does he explain how the principle of *uncertainty* would allow us to compress and encode information, which is precisely the issue in question. Indeed, the limitations of quantum computing may well be insurmountable, owing to the scaling problem (working with qubits rather than bits), the inevitability of quantum decoherence effects, the famous observation factor which can change quantum behavior, and the probabilistic nature of quantum solutions—what Brian Cox and Jeff Forshaw in *The Quantum Universe* call "ethereal quantum fluctuations." As science writer Jamie Condliffe admits in *Gizmodo*, "There isn't a huge amount of advantage in using a quantum computer compared to a regular one." Assuming that one could ever be built.

Moreover, quantum field theory suggests that the so-called wave/particle duality is not as cut and dried as Trudeau, the reporters and the audience seemed to believe. As physicist John Polkinghorne writes: "It turns out that in quantum field theory the states that show wavelike properties…are those that contain an *indefinite* number of particles." One would have to study the "wave equations" or at least dip into an explanatory text like Berezin's and Shubin's *The Schrödinger Equation* to plot how particles can propagate in the form of—wait for it—"*particle waves.*" Everything about the subject seems counter-intuitive. Ultimately, as Richard Feynman confessed in Volume III of *The Feynman Lectures on Physics*, "I think I can safely say that no one understands quantum mechanics"—not even, I would venture, Justin Trudeau.

I go on at some length about the quantum imbroglio because it furnishes an excellent example of Trudeau's glitzy superficiality. A skin-deep performer, he is good at looking the look and talking the talk, but at precious little else. Trudeau's manifold "accomplishments" surely have nothing to do with the intelligence and wisdom needed to govern a G7 nation. Mastering yoga poses, exhibiting snowboarding techniques, horsing around in a boxing ring, stripping for a ladies' charity function, or whiffling (in his case, glibly and without comprehension) on quantum computing are completely unrelated to an understanding of the thorny political and economic issues that go with responsible leadership in the turmoil of national and international affairs—apart from the fact that the dignity of statesmanship has gone by the board.

The truth is, I suspect, that Trudeau's public performances in the physical and intellectual domains, as well as his documented appeal to female effusiveness, is a vivid expression of his followers' utter lack of political sobriety, intellectual acumen and emotional maturity. That a country could give its support and a 66 per cent approval rating to a preening charlatan boggles the mind and beggars the imagination—or would, if Americans had not done the same with a smooth-talking ignoramus like Barack Obama, who thinks the U.S. consists of 57 states and that Austrians speak Austrian.

Canada has gone the way of the U.S. If it were not already obvious, it would take at least the eight limbs of *Samadhi* yogic meditation and petabytes of quantum computing to calculate the likelihood of such prodigious imbecility coming to pass, both in the leadership and the electorate, who appear to deserve one another. It makes me ashamed to be Canadian.

Feminism's Male Enablers

It is hard not to feel a certain *Schadenfreude* for that community of men in the universities and professions who are feminism's enablers, "femimen," as we may call them. These "white knights" have jumped on the feminist bandwagon in an excess of estrogen complicity, for a number of parallel reasons: career prospects, self-doubt, cultural acquiescence, fear of exclusion, docility of character, self-promotion, or sexual advantage. Some may even regard themselves as "survivors." I give three notable instances of the pathology at work.

Michael Kimmel is the founder of the journal *Men and Masculinities*, the voice of the National Organization for Men Against Sexism, Distinguished Professor of Sociology at Stony Brook, author of many popular books, and a committed feminist. His *Angry White Men: American Masculinity at the End of an Era*, described in his university bio as "a comparative study of the extreme right, White Supremacists, and neo-Nazis in the United States, Germany, and Scandinavia," has acquired near-legendary status. His reputation in the field of gender studies is immense and, until recently, untouchable. Now, Kimmel has himself been accused of sexual harassment, a case of a strenuous advocate for women's rights hoist with his own petard.

So far as I can tell, Kimmel is an unabashed and self-aggrandizing careerist who has never understood the lives of working men. He has thrived on his university authority, popular books and speaking engagements touting the need for understanding of and sensitivity to the plight of women on the part of men enslaved to their own raw and turbulent masculinity. Though he assumes the mantle of enlightened fairness, I regard him as a fraud who has done much harm in promoting the social and cultural dysfunction from which we now suffer. There is a kind of poetic justice in his recent troubles. Naturally, Kimmel immediately played the apology card and lobbied for survival by wishing to "make amends to those who believe I have injured them." The creepy and patently insincere mawkishness of this star feminist is par for the course. Kimmel is not to be pitied, nor is the feminist sorority to be pardoned. They are equally complicit in acts of malfeasance.

One thinks, too, of Steven Galloway, formerly a professor at the University of British Columbia, author of the international bestseller *The Cellist of Sarajevo*, and a member in good standing of Canada's politically correct literary community, who found himself fired by his university and cast into outer darkness on the basis of demonstrably false accusations of sexual misconduct. Although cleared of all charges by an independent inquiry, he was not reinstated. He has no future prospects in this country, neither as a writer nor a professor.

Yet he has admitted to participating in rejecting a job application from a candidate to his department owing to an unproven sexual allegation against the applicant by a female graduate student, indicating Galloway's career-driven or inner assent to the reigning feminist orthodoxy. But the issue was rather more complicated than appeared at first sight. It turns out he had been having an extramarital affair with the same graduate student who had made the initial allegation against the hapless applicant, and who was now, in a crowning irony, accusing her mentor and lover of rape. Galloway's long and meandering text in the *National Post*, partly an exercise in *mea culpa* and partly an exculpatory document, will not serve to extricate him from the feminist dungeon. Nor does it excuse his naivety, his desire to believe without evidence. Some men never seem to learn.

Jian Ghomeshi, formerly a celebrity broadcaster for the CBC, was the target of a lying campaign by a gaggle of unscrupulous women who accused him of sexual abuse. Though exonerated in a famous trial in which his accusers were shown to have colluded in preparing a sheaf of false charges — some of whom continued wanting to date him even at the time of his alleged misconduct — his career is ruined and his reputation in tatters. "I've become a hashtag," he says.

Ghomeshi in his own words had been "a doctrinaire activist who was tear-gassed at protests." He wore T-shirts "screaming slogans of equality and liberation." And he admits to having used his "liberal gender studies as a cover for my own behavior." Although he quite justifiably "cannot confess to the accusations that are inaccurate," he now feels "deep remorse about how I treated some people in my life." He affirms that he is "not suddenly an antifeminist activist, stage-diving at a *Breitbart* road show" and goes so far as to say that he now sees his own actions "as part of a systemic culture of unhealthy masculinity." Though I believe he may be sincere in his expression of contrition, Ghomeshi has clearly made all the right penitential moves in a well-written but humiliating apology for his dismissive and narcissistic conduct—chiefly with women, obviously. It doesn't make any difference.

"Men seem to be so cowed that they can't fight back," said former feminist Doris Lessing. This is doubly true of feminism's advocates or allies. They do not fight back, they apologize and repent. They may claim they have reformed, they may acknowledge bad behavior, they may salvage a few shreds of dignity by showing how they have been slandered and misprized, they may be vindicated in law or by inquiry, and they may swear not to disavow their feminist sympathies, but it does them no good. All the virtue-signalling in the world will not help to redeem a perceived transgression or permanently remove the stigma. Better these men should never have been feminist enablers, opportunistic sympathizers or go-along trendies in the first place. Compliant men, take heed. Feminist *bona fides* count for nothing in the breach.

Kimmel, Galloway and Ghomeshi are representative figures indulging a talent for maudlin regrets in a bid to atone for a wayward but not uncommon sex life. Apologizing for natural male vigor and energy in violation of their own inherent masculinity is a form of psychological suicide. Indeed, the onus falls equally on women who tend to appreciate virile men and who enter into relationships knowing full well what they are doing. Men are men and women are women and that is realistically all there is to it.

Begging forgiveness for being a man is precisely the kind of saccharine reparation that Iron John wouldn't be caught dead making. As poet Robert Bly writes in his book of that title, "Contact with Iron John requires a willingness to descend into the male psyche and accept what's dark down there, including the *nourishing* dark." There should be no temporizing. Moreover, men should recognize that feminism does not tolerate what we might call indemnity politics on the part of its fellow-traveling victims. The shaming industry is relentless and the Twitter mobs are ruthless. An allegation is always a verdict in the feminist mind, as it is for the madding crowd of the social media world.

The truth is, no one is safe from the feminist blitz, not even its male collaborators. After all, despite their unmanly support for or deference to the cause, they too are men. It is unfortunate that politics, career or emotional rapport has led them to forget that fact.

On Scented Minipads

Before I invested in a car one of the most harrowing experiences I had to submit to daily was the rush-hour bus or metro. It wasn't the waiting in line, the hideous crush of humanity, the standing for what seemed like hours that particularly distressed me, it was the smell. There is nothing quite so devastating as the stench of coagulating deodorants. People smelled like rancid chocolate. I especially remember the cumulative shock wave of Old Spice which made my nostrils crumple like newspaper. But that was only the men. The women were in another olfactory dimension entirely. The odor of wilted gardenia was omnipresent. I would stand beside pretty young women who stank like urinal pucks of rosewater, sandalwood and antiseptic. Others smelled like perambulating lemons, acrid, with a hint of Windex lingering about their persons. It was worse in the early mornings when people reeked like corpses doused with the failed discretion of embalming fluid. Now and then there would rise in the air a suspicion of fart fledged with the ethereal plumage of Chanel or Fabergé. That was how I knew these slumped unmoving forms were still alive.

I wonder what it is we are ashamed of. Is Old Spice the child of the New Testament? Is Lady Speed Stick the lineal descendant of Pauline theology? Do all these gels and applications confess to a secret contempt for the flesh as being somehow too primitive, too pagan, too animal, too unruly, too *present*? We enjoy our bodies too much to give them up. A passionate fling, a pneumatic eiderdown, coffee and oranges in a sunny chair (to quote Wallace Stevens), the long, easy, meditative, peristaltic flex of the bowels—who can deny such experiences are inherently pleasurable? Yet hundreds of years of Presbyterianism are not flung aside with a Belmondo shrug. When everything has been factored out by historical analysis, there remains the guilt. The old resentment of the body continues to rankle and fester but the intransigent love of the body persists with countervailing strength. From this tension, this conflict, the cosmetics industry has always profited.

Today we need no longer splash perfumes about indiscriminately to make up for the lack of sanitary facilities. Everybody in the civilized world can enjoy at least a simple ablution at almost any moment of the day or night. One might think if there ever were a time in which deodorants should appeal to nobody but perverts, it would be right now. Yet the opposite is the case. Could the reason be that as the manifold delights of the flesh become more and more available, the endocrinology of guilt abides with us even more tenaciously. Thus the deodorant explosion. We have bodies but we don't have bodies. We become our own fragrant Gardens of Eden. We are the resurrected flesh promised by the Book of Revelation and the Koran.

The scented minipad, however, is a unique symbol of our existential condition. One can scarcely turn on the TV these days without seeing some nubile ballerina in mid-splits expatiating on the virtues of the latest in yoniwear. It reposes invisibly beneath her tutu like a hospital tuck, clean and decisive. It permits her to solve the occupational hazard of being a woman and to quell the monthly tremors of the professional ballet dancer. Not only can she perform the most strenuous of cabrioles without bleeding like a stuck pig but she even smells sweetly afterwards. Now she can be a man and a flower at the same time.

The scented minipad—to widen the conjecture—derives not only from our inheritance of guilt before the unassimilable mortification of the flesh—Original Skin, as it were—but from the apologetic dis-ease women feel before their own raw femininity. The minipad betokens the compound transgression of having not just a body but, O mater Dolorosa! a female body. Sweat, feces and menarche are difficult enough for any sensitive being to put up with, but discharge too! And so women run about in a state of aromatic nether purdah whose eventual disclosure leads to the most unfortunate of after-effects. I know of men who, following acts of glossal intimacy, have been reduced to repeated and obsessive gargling to recover the use of their taste buds. Any man who has managed to hang on to his senses would rather part an honest patch of pubic hair than enter a grove of synthetic pomegranates or visit a well-kept cemetery redolent of the ghosts of departed minipads.

There is, of course, a practical side to the scented minipad—apart from the soothing of catamenial despairs—which is more than an expression of ancestral guilt. It is also a way of disguising a more immediate one. The scented minipad is the latest flower of sin. As sex becomes less confined to the prudence of the night and grows increasingly diurnal, women must not only keep themselves on red alert but come home smelling of inoffensive lilac. They are cleansed not only of having flesh but of using it. But this is a mere quotidian advantage that does not disguise a deeper hankering for salvation.

The TV commercials reveal what it is we really long for. The verbal gush coupled with the vaginal stanch are no different in principle from the manly reticence cloaked in English Leather commanding the velocity flow of a black RX-7. This is how it will manifestly be in Heaven where we shall all enjoy the paradisiacal disembarrassment of our natural awkwardness. We shall be in total control of our fears and secretions, acting with the assurance of disembodiment. Meanwhile the Great Panegyric is flourishing as never before and the whited sepulchre, as is only proper in this day of rampant miniaturization, has become portable and ubiquitous.

A Is Not for Activist

It is dispiriting to note that those to whom we have entrusted the education of our children in the primary and public schools are woefully under-educated practitioners of the discipline. In an article titled *Educational Rot*, Walter Williams laments "the low academic quality of so many teachers." Williams is referring to the abomination of teacher training colleges, which recruit the dregs of the graduate schools, catering to candidates "who have the lowest academic test scores." The same applies to graduates of the Gender Studies programs in the universities who, unfit for productive employment, will often end up in the K-12 classroom. The damage such instructors do to the public school system and to our children is incalculable.

Trained to follow a Left curricular agenda, a majority of K-12 teachers are set on molding the social justice warriors, anti-free market revolutionaries, radical environmentalists, global warmists and feminist Furies of the future. The exclusion of the traditional focus on writing skills, effective reading, civics, maths and sciences, and the counter-emphasis on "social justice" themes in the public schools constitutes the first stage of the systematic dumbing down—what historian Niall Ferguson calls *The Great Degeneration*—that afflicts our society.

Thus, far too many students who emerge from these incubators, whether they are conscious of it or not, suffer not only from mental sluggishness but from a kind of psychic immiseration. They compensate by trying to persuade themselves that they are useful and enlightened citizens when, for the most part, they are merely antisocial drones. The gene pool is not being chlorinated, as Wendy Northcutt suggests in her 2009 Darwin Awards romp; on the contrary, it is being increasingly contaminated.

Inspired by the reigning cultural ideology and Left political legislation, our K-12 purveyors of the Progressivist meme have put into practice the adage attributed to St. Ignatius Loyola (though possibly mischievously mis-assigned to him by Voltaire): "Give me a child until he is seven and I will show you the man." There is much truth in the saying, as Aristotle recognized in Book 7 of the *Politics*, arguing that children should be reared in the home until the critical age of seven when their instincts will have been shaped and characters formed. After this developmental mission has been completed, children proceed to the "Lessons," that is, music and gymnastics, before moving to the higher echelons as they prepare to begin the journey into adulthood.

Of course, Aristotle was concerned with raising good citizens, sound of body and mind, willing to defend the polis from its enemies, and able to reflect dispassionately on social and political issues. Our pedagogues have a different purpose in mind. The citizens they wish to create are agenda-driven ideologues who believe their own country, to quote New York governor Andrea Cuomo, "was never that great,"—indeed it is the sum of all evil—and that what we may call "identity tribalism" is the road forward to true egalitarianism.

Even toddlers are not spared the rigors of indoctrination. Consider the profound imbecility of a kiddie text like *C is for Consent*, in which young children are taught about "body boundaries" and personal choice in giving and receiving affection. If Grandpa leans down to kiss his grandson, "Mom says, 'Please ask for consent first.'" Believe it! That the author Eleanor Morrison is a #MeToo adherent tells us all we need to know. My grandmother always kissed me and gave me a dollar. I could have wished for two of each.

These poor abused children are regularly subjected to board books like *A is for Activist*, in which after a series of atrocious rhymes they are bombarded with asinine slogans they can barely understand, like "Environmental justice is the way!" and "Creative Counter to Corporate Vultures." They are asked "Are you an Activist?" By the age of seven, the answer to the question is probably: Yes.

And by the time they reach university, a staggering number of them are fundamentally dysfunctional, devoid of basic knowledge and convinced they must repudiate and undo the presumed sins of their fathers. They cannot write a coherent English sentence, will agitate for LGBTQ+ rights, will shout down conservative speakers and denounce "white supremacism," will don masks and battle gear to disrupt public events, and profess a passionate dedication to the most destructive of political philosophies, universal socialism. K-12 is a slough of didactic despond, turning out largely illiterate and innumerate fodder for the universities and foot soldiers for the coming revolution. Its charges do not consist of pupils but recruits.

As educator Ken Poppe, a veteran of 47 years in the trenches, writes in his as yet unpublished memoir, *If I Ran My School*, "all the red tape paperwork, the government interference, the political correctness, the constant threat of litigation, the gross misallocation of money—even the suspicion by co-workers if you got too good—left me thinking it's nearly impossible for any neophyte to rise above all this." And he is right. Trying to bring public education back to the summit it once occupied is a Sisyphean task.

Plainly, home-schooling will be an uphill battle as, for example, the Canadian comedy film *Adventures in Public Schooling* makes abundantly clear. The film tells the story of a home-schooled prodigy who escapes his mother's stifling over-parenting and enters the broader, socially-hip and far more interesting realm of the public school. *Variety* reviewer Dennis Harvey, while clearly deploring home-schooling, generously acknowledges that the mother is at least "not serving some extreme religious or political agenda"—an attitude that represents the common perception of the phenomenon. The film concludes with a reconciliation between mother and son. The mother, says Harvey, may have been an "overzealous best friend," but, thank the Lord, was not "a terrifying example of pathological dependency and transference"—again, an attitude that expresses how the home-schooling parent is generally regarded.

Adventures in Public Schooling manages to hide the reality of mediocrity and indoctrination that characterizes the public school system under a veneer of lighthearted ebullience.

Nevertheless, steps must be taken to redeem the K-12 disaster, for that is what it truly is. It needs to be admitted that K-12 education cannot be reformed, it must be replaced. Vouchers, charter schools and home schooling should be encouraged and parental choice, responsibility and authority must supersede the intrusion of self-interested bureaucracies in the educational process. There would be no Teachers Unions. Once necessary to ensure job security and decent salaries, they inevitably become Club Meds for Union officials and bastions of professional mediocrity. They will no longer figure in the new dispensation. Teachers Training Colleges will be a thing of the past; teachers will be drawn solely from their respective disciplines, which they will be expected to have mastered. The insinuation of political theories and ideological practices into the minds of the young will be strictly prohibited.

The only solution that has a chance of success is the empowerment of the parent and the home and the elimination of a top-heavy, inefficient and wasteful educational bureaucracy. Of course, such would be a slow and intermittent process, failing which ongoing academic—and cultural—decline is inevitable.

A happy and well-educated child is the optimum goal for early education. That such an aim is conspicuous by its absence and remains differentially elusive should not deter us from the struggling to achieve it as best we can. In the long run, happiness comes with work, integrity, self-respect and mental discipline. These are qualities which the institutional monolith cannot foster.

Indeed, as Aristotle wrote in the *Nichomachean Ethics*, happiness, as the purpose of life, relies on fostering moral reason and intellectual excellence, for which the Greek word is *arête*. As the philosopher knew, the concept is central to true education and must begin with the young.

A is not for Activist. A is for *arête*.

Hockey Has Gone South

I grew up, like many if not most Canadians, passionately in love with hockey. As a child, I listened on my bedside radio to Danny Gallivan, the best hockey announcer bar none, call the Montreal Canadiens games in his unmistakable Cape Bretonish twang. I can still recall jumping up and down in sheer delirium whenever the Canadiens (known affectionately as the Habs, after the French *Habitants*) scored a goal, and especially when my boyhood hero Boom Boom Geoffrion, who got his nickname from the sound of his slapshot cannonading off the boards, scorched the puck into the net. My mother would enter the room with a glass of warm milk to calm me down.

My teen ambition was to become the Habs goaltender. Playing against rural teams in the north of Quebec, I still bear the scars, a chipped tooth (the result of a "great save") and a few other faded marks of those youthful exploits. But it was not to be. I suspected I was simply not good enough to pursue that dream and, besides, university studies were far too demanding in that era to allow for adolescent compulsions.

My devotion to the game has since waned. *Les Canadiens — nos amours* and *nos glorieux* as Quebeckers refer to the team — were once a great hockey franchise, with a record 24 Stanley Cups to their credit. I'm still nostalgic for the days when general manager Sam Pollock worked his magic, steering the Canadiens to dynastic eminence. Pollock lived beside two celebrated Canadian poets, Doug Jones and Ralph Gustafson in North Hatley, Quebec, and probably imbibed their influence, or perhaps vice versa. Robust imaginations and dedication to their respective crafts were something they had in common. The stern perfectionist and brilliant strategist Scotty Bowman was coach, the last of a stellar succession that included Cecil Hart, Dick Irvin and Toe Blake. Under Bowman's stewardship, the 1976-77 Canadiens became the most dominant team in sports history, suffering only 8 losses in a 70 game season.

Since that heady time, with only few exceptions, it's been pretty much downhill. The Canadien organization gradually became the Bermuda Triangle of the hockey world. Myopic ownership, defective management, incompetent coaches, poor drafting and disastrous trades resulted in thirty years of generally lackluster performance. The decline of the team is also politically unfortunate. The Canadiens were one of the few binding influences in a province divided by the "two solitudes," Franco and Anglo, and by economic disparity. D'Arcy Jenish in his *The Montreal Canadiens: 100 Years of Glory*, shows how hockey could work as a source of political rapprochement between estranged cultural and linguistic constituents. Regrettably, the "Flying Frenchmen" are now grounded.

The National Hockey League (NHL), too, despite a number of superstars and a couple of exciting teams, has deteriorated largely as a consequence of runaway expansion into the vast American market, swelling eventually from the original six teams to thirty, now thirty-one with the addition of the Las Vegas Golden Knights and soon to be thirty-two with a Seattle franchise. The pool of local talent has not been sufficient to stock the rosters, hence the importation of an army of European players transforming the League into a kind of United Nations, a Global Village on ice. Half the players bear names that defy pronunciation and, sewn on the back of their jerseys, are practically indecipherable. This would be acceptable or even desirable to many—the idea of one-worldism come to fruition—but the sense of local attachment, of a kind of patriotism, has been seriously diluted, making it hard to recognize one's native game. Hockey is a more insular game than, say, baseball or soccer.

Moreover, the players are so padded, face-shielded and helmeted as to resemble *Star Wars* characters. The goaltenders are like tanks on skates; to be successful in today's league, they must be well over six feet tall. The Vancouver Canucks recruited John McLean, who at 6'9" and 205 pounds need merely remain immobile to achieve success in the nets. The great goaltenders who came before, all maskless and wearing skimpier equipment—Terry Sawchuck, Sugar Ray Henry, Harry Lumley, even shot-peppered Al Rollins of the sad sack Chicago Blackhawks—could likely outperform any of their contemporary counterparts.

The great players of yore, all helmetless—Maurice "the rocket" Richard, Gordie Howe, Red Kelly, Jean Béliveau (*le Gros Bill*), Andy Bathgate, Larry Robinson, Bobby Orr, Guy "the Flower" Lafleur, Wayne "the Great One" Gretzky (helmetless until the 1979 League helmet ruling), among others—whizzed and stickhandled around the rink, unencumbered by burdensome accoutrements. "We didn't wear helmets or face shields back then," writes Béliveau in his memoir *My Life in Hockey*, "so our sticks were carried at ice level most of the time." Hockey sticks were not Kevlar-and-graphite weapons intended to mutilate opposing players. Tripping, hooking, slashing, or hitting from behind were frowned upon. Brawling was a sideshow, not a staple as in today's game. Scrums along the boards were whistled down to prevent boredom. The tedious dump-and-chase syndrome was far less frequent than carrying the puck into the offensive zone. Skill, flair, speed and on-ice personality were favored, unlike today's Rollerball antics. It was, to cite a phrase, a beautiful game.

Even worse, not only has the NHL adulterated its quality along with its identity, a development accelerated by League commissioner, the smarmy and diminutive Gary Bettman, it appears to have grown at least marginally corrupt, or so it seems to many of its increasingly disenchanted fans and those who remember its best days. It is, of course, much harder to fix a hockey game than, say, a boxing match, but the operation is theoretically possible via subtle hints and coded instructions to the referees.

Of course, other team sports are not immune to misfeasance. NBA referee Tim Donaghy betting on games and manipulating the point spread between teams was a scandal with which the Association itself was not involved — though Donaghy claims that "Special players get ... special treatment, and that's just the craft of officiating in the NBA." And one recalls the egregious and glaringly obvious non-call in the 2019 NFC championship game that arguably cost the small-market New Orleans Saints a win against the large-market Los Angeles Rams.

The most recent example of possible National Hockey League jobbery stems from the 2017 Stanley Cup quarter-final playoffs between the Edmonton Oilers and the Anaheim Ducks. The refs bungled two glaring goaltender interference incidents and botched an offside and an icing call, which led to Anaheim goals. As a result, Anaheim won the games in question and eventually clinched the series. How could several consecutive instances of presumed incompetence have happened? The issue of "confirmation bias," in which the Situation Room in Toronto reviews controversial calls of the officials, may play into occasions of this nature; the command center generally confirms the referees in order not to embarrass them. But the problem may go deeper than that.

My hockey friends speculate that the League could not tolerate two Canadian teams, in this case the Oilers and the surprising Ottawa Senators, meeting in the Cup finals. American viewership would dwindle to insignificance, TV ratings would plummet, and advertising revenues would go, well, not south but north, a fiscal catastrophe to be avoided at all costs. One Canadian team is a viable proposition, but two? Consequently, according to the cynical — or skeptical — view, at least one of the Canadian teams had to be eliminated. This could explain what might otherwise remain inexplicable, namely, how four game officials and a Situation Room majority could err so dramatically *call after call* to the clear advantage of one team over another. I can't vouch for the hypothesis, but the argument does make sense.

Reputedly adapted from Irish hurling as hurley-on-ice in the province of Nova Scotia in the late 18th century, hockey is — or was — a Canadian game. The four American teams of the original six — New York, Boston, Chicago, Detroit — were all reasonably close to the border and a short jaunt to Montreal and Toronto. They seemed to us Canadian by proxy. Further, they depended on a Canadian player base. The Stanley Cup, the oldest trophy in North American professional sports, is named after Lord Frederick Arthur Stanley, appointed by Queen Victoria as Governor General of Canada in 1888. The NHL got its start in 1917 in the small Ontario town of Renfrew; it has met its end as a credible institution in rampant over-extension, extraterritoriality and the profitable glitz of the modern American hockey/TV market.

The continuing affection many fans feel for their teams is understandable, but the sport itself has been compromised—merely another aspect of the intellectual, cultural and political mediocrity that characterizes our time. Everywhere we look the desideratum of quality is growing less and less observable. Now that the League has become a caricature and the game a free-for-all, it requires something like religious faith or civic loyalty to keep on rooting for the colors. A beautiful game is no longer quite so beautiful.

The Unbearable Whiteness of Being

There can be little doubt that the modern university, in its obsession with race, gender and sexual orientation under the rubric of "social justice," has violated its core mandate which, in the words of Matthew Arnold from *Culture and Anarchy*, is to familiarize readers and students with "the best that has been thought and said." The Academy has turned Arnold's maxim on its head, instructing students in the worst that has been thought and said—and done. The curricular fetish of "social justice," which is destroying the university as an institution of higher learning, continues to metastasize.

Indeed, the university as a social and cultural institution is a slow-motion train wreck picking up speed: equity hiring, affirmative action, anti-conservative and overt leftist politics, the "diversity and inclusion" myth on which the Academy prides itself, group think, speech codes, snitch lines, trigger warnings, safe spaces, microaggressions, the attack on academic freedom—the list goes on.

The bogus issue that has recently acquired major prominence in the quagmire of campus politics is "whiteness," especially the "hegemony" of straight white males and their champions, guilty, apparently, of every conceivable ill that has bedeviled the world since the first silverback emerged from the jungle. This is merely a prime manifestation of the reigning hysteria on college campuses, in particular its mephitic obsession with race. "The toxic racial climate of colleges looks to be perpetual," warns Scott Greer in *No Campus for White Men*; anti-white ferocity "remains established as an unchallenged dogma." There is no campus for some white woman as well. Witness the current vendetta against distinguished University of Chicago Medievalist Rachel Fulton Brown.

Notes from a Derelict Culture

The author of a blog post "Three Cheers for White Men," a committed Catholic and a lover of Western civilization and its Christian foundations as her many books confirm, Fulton Brown has been vilified as a Nazi and a hater. For daring to defend western Christendom as the source of many of our most cherished values of gender equality and respect for individual worth, she has been cross-haired by a mob of professors of Literature, History, and Medieval Studies who are determined to destroy her professionally, writing an open letter to her university, festooned with 1500 signatures and stating that she is a disgrace to the history department.

The intent of the open letter is clearly to have Fulton Brown fired or at least disciplined. She is reviled as a white supremacist spreading heteropatriarchal desecrations—a perfect example of "motive attribution asymmetry" as defined in a 2014 article in *The Proceedings of the National Academy of Sciences*. One's enemies deserve only contempt since they are irremediably evil and intractable. Although the study suggests that "fundamental cognitive bias" and "outgroup hate" can be mitigated by adopting certain incentives, this does not seem to be the case when it comes to the Left. The profanity hurled against Fulton Brown on Twitter by a presumably cultivated professoriate is unprintable, fit only for the lower depths. As Richard Mitchell aptly wrote in *The Graves of Academe*, "The prodigious monster is down there."

Naturally, the fact that the entire infrastructure these gutter academics take for granted—the electrical grid that lights their libraries and offices, the buildings in which they sit and type their treatises, the roads they drive on and the planes they fly in, the Twitter feeds and Facebook posts that facilitate their frenzied denunciations of those they deem beyond the pale, the medications that keep them going, the food they put on the table, the table they put under the food, the vintage wines they sip in the faculty lounge, the plumbing on which they rely, the physical and technical maintenance that enables them to survive, the accessories of any sort they assume as given, indeed, just about *everything*—is due to the labor, ingenuity, risk and entrepreneurial innovation of mainly straight white males of European and American provenance and to the uniformly despised capitalist enterprise.

The Unbearable Whiteness of Being

In focusing on the Fulton Brown fiasco, I will surely be accused by detractors of cherry picking, but any observer willing to do the research will find that the entire cherry orchard is tainted, scarcely a healthy drupe to be found. *Globe and Mail* columnist Doug Saunders, for example, derides such reports of university malfeasance, claiming "To mistake a colourful anecdote for a measurable trend is a basic scholarly mistake." The instance I've cited, however, is not anomalous but symptomatic. Saunders should know better. The mistake is his, either an expression of profound ignorance or a deliberate lie.

As Milo Yiannopoulos writes in a major defense of Fulton Brown, an inquisition is underway led by an army of self-proclaimed "arbiters of moral taste, determined to rid the field of infidels." They are intent on "burning the witch." Fulton Brown's heresy is her affirmation that the study of the Middle Ages "is fundamental to understanding how the Christian West emerged, and how dramatically its character differs from other cultures," which explains the current moral panic about white supremacy presumably associated with the period. "But the most absurd dimension of it all," Yiannopoulos continues, "is that nothing associates the Middle Ages with white supremacy more than journalists and academics shrieking about it."

In his seminal volume *White Guilt*, black scholar Shelby Steele deplores the consequences of what he calls *dissociational* thinking, the academic tendency to dissociate excellence and truth from a marketable conception of social virtue and justice and to regard race and ethnicity — non-white, of course — as meritorious in themselves. Excellence has become irrelevant as whiteness, the target of motive attribution asymmetry, has become sinister. Dissociation, Steele concludes, "is a power that always works by eroding the quality of the host institution" while creating a "vacuum of moral authority at the center of American life."

To be white, Christian and proud of one's heritage is now the kiss of death. Rachel Fulton Brown, an excellent scholar and a woman of high moral character, is the most recent victim of the dissociational bigotry that governs the university environment. She won't be the last.

Re-Interpreting the Koran

As I've written on several previous occasions, there exists a sect of reformist Muslims who believe that the Koran has been grievously misread by cavillers and doubters who are convinced that Islam is not a religion of peace, but a violent and imperialistic faith intent on world conquest. The passages in the Koran—and the environing literature as well—that give rise to the animosity of nit-pickers and quibblers, the enlightened Muslims claim, require to be re-interpreted so that their temperate and merciful essence can be made plain to all.

Embarking on the process of re-interpretation can be a salutary and liberating task, one that we spurn at the peril of darkest ignorance and counter-productive rancor. Eventually the detractors of Islam may realize that they have failed to grasp the beauty, elegance and rhetoric of conciliation that animate the holy texts and be moved to make amends for their anti-Islamic vitriol and stubborn recidivism.

To consider only a few salient instances of controversial passages that have been consistently misapprehended:

Koran 2:191, speaking of infidels who do not accept the word of the Prophet, commands us to "kill them wherever you may find them." Here we must be particularly alert, subtle and astute, for killing the unbelievers does not mean to slay them bodily, but to kill them with kindness, in other words, to shower the candy of life upon them, to reward them with prestigious appointments and lavish emoluments, to bow before them in the streets and welcome them into the homes of the devout, to address them with profound respect, to decorate them with titles and ply them with accolades—until, bedazzled by the nobility and magnanimity of Islam, they are ready to convert.

Similarly, in Koran 2:216, where we read that "fighting is prescribed" for the faithful, we are to understand that the battle is enjoined to vanquish the evil impulse in Muslim and non-Muslim alike, until universal harmony and jubilation dominate the world. This is the true meaning and purpose of the Caliphate. News stories of ISIS fighters decapitating prisoners are clearly fake news. ISIS fighters are obviously misunderstood benefactors of humanity, lovers of Christians, Jews and atheists, as well as ardent feminists.

When Allah warns in Koran 3:56, with regard to those who reject the faith, "I will punish them with terrible agony," the Supreme Lord does not propose insupportable physical torment but, rather, the moral suffering that comes from the recognition of apostasy or denial, which can only strengthen the fibre of a mortified conscience.

Koran 5:33 informs us that "The punishment of those who wage war against Allah and His messenger and strive to make mischief in the land is only this, that they should be murdered or crucified or their hands and their feet should be cut off on opposite sides or they should be imprisoned; this shall be as a disgrace for them in this world, and in the hereafter they shall have a grievous chastisement."

Admittedly, this is hard verse to fathom; however, as is often the Prophet's wont, he is not targeting body parts but engaging in graphic allegory to impress upon both believers and unbelievers the self-torture they will feel, smitten by their higher selves, should they curse the Almighty.

In the same way, Koran 8:12, which reads: "I will cast terror into the hearts of those who disbelieve. Therefore strike off their heads and strike off every fingertip of them," is not meant to be taken literally. The true meaning is: browbeat them tactfully and lightly slap their wrists if they persist in their folly and continue to rebuff your acts of philanthropic munificence. This is the Islamic version of tough love.

Koran 18:65-81 is often taken to condone honor killing, since what appears to be the senseless murder of a young man is only meant to spare his parents the trauma of his imminent misdeeds and to prepare the way for a successor. Of course, one knows that killing is frowned upon in Muslim culture, and this apparent killing of the young man is nothing but the symbolic correlate of expunging his "disobedience" and mischief-making and replacing his wayward sensibility with contrition and the promise of rehabilitation.

Koran 47:35 adjures: "Be not weary and faint-hearted, crying for peace, when you should have the upper hand, for Allah is with you." The "upper hand" (Arabic: *shakir*) refers not to arrogant predominance or to the hand that strikes downward from the crown to the jaw, cleaving the skull in two, but to the hand that is raised heavenward in prayer.

The same procedure leading to the extraction of authentic purport applies, for example, to the Hadith as well (sayings and acts ascribed to Mohammed). For example:

When, in *Bukhari* 11:626, Mohammed discloses that "I decided to order a man to lead the prayer and then take a flame to burn all those who had not left their houses for the prayer, burning them alive inside their homes," he does not envision the burning of the flesh but the inward fire of self-contempt that slackers and tergiversators will eventually experience. The pain of remorse can indeed be searing.

In *Bukhari* 52:177, we read that "the Hour [of Resurrection] will not be established until you fight with the Jews." This admonition obviously has nothing to do with anti-Semitism; the idea is to engage in playful sparring and amiable argumentation with Jews in order to reveal the high spirits, good humor and self-deprecating modesty of Islam, thus impressing the initially skeptical Jews with the genial nature and friendly feelings inherent in the faith.

Analogously, when we find in *Ibn Ishaq/Hisham* 9:90 the divine behest that "A prophet must slaughter before collecting captives," neither the term "slaughter" nor "captives" connotes anything malevolent or untoward. "Slaughter" refers to animal sacrifice in homage to the deity; "captives" alludes not to slavery, an abomination which critics of Islam unfairly accuse it of practicing even to this day, but to the human heart binding itself in the golden chains of celestial beatitude.

Thus, when Mohammed, in *Tabari* 9:69, is reported as saying that "Killing unbelievers is a small matter to us," we come to understand that this is among the most pacific of passages in the Hadith. By "unbelievers," Mohammed is once again drawing attention to animal sacrifice on the altar of devotion, for animals do not believe or worship. And by "a small matter," Mohammed, a master ironist, is merely being facetious. The "small matter" is clearly of gravest importance, the carrying out of certain ritual decrees regarding the treatment of animals, which today justify the custom of *halal* cuisine.

Again, those who are strangers to nuance will misconstrue a text like *Muslim* 19: 4294, in which we are told that "When the Messenger of Allah (may peace be upon him) appointed anyone as leader of an army or detachment he would especially exhort him [to] make a holy war." A reset is needed if we are to grasp the Prophet's tenor, for by prosecuting holy war, we are to understand righteous preaching for the benefit of the human soul. No one is to get hurt for Islam is the religion of peace, amity and concord.

I have isolated merely a sparse handful of the myriad comparable passages and tropes that proliferate throughout the Islamic canon. The same habit of re-interpretation—which is actually proper interpretation—of the scriptures is the *sine qua non* for reading and understanding the traditional texts of Islam. Indeed, every venomous, inflammatory or disturbingly ambiguous passage in the entire range of Islamic writings, counsels, messages and prescriptions, when placed in the appropriate light, can be seen to denote the opposite. We are all *dhimmis*, second class beings, compared to the Creator. We must all pay the *jizzya*, or tribute tax, of genuine worship to the Lord of the Universe. We discover our freedom in "perfect slavery" (a term popularized by the medieval Islamic scholars al-Qushayri and Ibn Arabi) to the dictates of an enlightened conscience and ethical behavior. Life is a blessing and a miracle, which the *Sharia*, by ordering our activities down to the minutest details, confirms and extols—*Sharia* may look like totalitarian compulsion but it is really perfect love. "Submission" is the triumphal assertion of the sanctified will, that is, submission to our best selves, aka our Islamic selves. Beheading ("smiting of the neck") is only a metaphor for changing one's mind about first and last things. And so on.

It is only the literalists, the barbarians, the uneducated, and the unevolved among Muslims who will act in defiance of their sacred texts, even if they happen to constitute a majority. They are patently unable to process what any sensitive and informed person among the *ummah*—or for that matter, among Jews, Christians and secular Westerners—recognizes immediately: the Koran and its outriders are not what they appear to be to primitive, malicious and uninstructed minds. What seems opaque or problematic becomes instantly transparent to an agile and sympathetic intelligence. For there is no violence or niggardliness in Islam, only light, majesty and infinite tolerance for suffering mankind. This is the charm of the initially paradoxical passage in Koran 5:54: "O believers, take not Jews and Christians as friends; they are friends of each other. Those of you who make them his friends is one of them. God does not guide an unjust people." By which Mohammed means that one should embrace the foreigner not simply as a friend but as a more-than-friend, a brother, a soul mate, in short, as one cherishes one's own spirit. Otherwise, one will be in dire want of divine guidance.

We owe a debt of gratitude to the school of enlightened and panoptic Muslim thinkers, editors and redactors without whom we would remain trapped in a tangle of misconceptions respecting the religion of peace. It is time we gave it its due.

The Blue Lobster

One of the more piquant news stories of the last few days reports the capture of a rare blue lobster off the north shore of Canada's Prince Edward Island. In the maritime world this is an almost unprecedented find, a crustacean with a genetic disorder, destined not for the table but the aquarium. In the political and intellectual worlds, however, blue lobsters — unlike black swans — abound. They surface everywhere one gazes, swarming into the nets of history, clambering among the reefs of contemporary events, brandishing their pincers, drawing attention to the extravagant pigmentation of which they are inordinately proud. Despite its electric sheen, the ventings of this arthropod sensibility, so oddly articulated and living within its impermeable shell, should by this time no longer provoke wonderment.

One of these more notable blue lobsters is George Friedman, a prime representative of his class. Founder and editor of the increasingly influential intelligence corporation Stratfor, Friedman has begun to weigh in on global affairs with a veritable plethora of articles, digests, summaries and evaluations. To be sure, at times he can make reasonably good sense; but all too often, as with many of his pixilated species, his analyses are so bizarre as to put one off one's appetite for research into public affairs entirely.

For example, his suggestion that a way out of the Iranian morass would be for the U.S. to pursue an alliance with Ayatollah Khamenei. "From the American standpoint, an understanding with Iran would have the advantage of solving an increasingly knotty problem," he opines. Just as Stalin and Mao were not really "crazy," as popular wisdom had it, and therefore could be engaged by Roosevelt and Nixon respectively, so an Iranian panjandrum can be regarded as more of a rhetorical windbag than a man of action or a man of his word, and can be successfully approached by the U.S. with a view to furthering their mutual interests. The sheer unworldliness of his assessment leaves the reader wondering if Friedman is living on the same planet as the rest of us. (Though, on second thought, it must be admitted he did keep company to some extent with the Obama administration, which had more than its share of blue lobsters.)

The same can be said of his appraisal of the Israeli/Palestinian quandary and the vexed issue of establishing final borders. Friedman allows *pro forma* that "There is a strong case for not returning to the 1949 lines," but as *Israpundit*'s Ted Belman notes, "'He doesn't make the case." I would hazard that the reason he doesn't make the case is that there is no case to be made. He is willing to offer a brief gesture of conciliation to those who might disagree with him but, having demonstrated his apparent open-mindedness, retracts his concession almost immediately in order to proceed with his argument.

Like many of his fellow blue lobsters (who for some weird motive tend to be obsessed with Israel), Friedman insists that the country would be best served by retreating to the pre-1967 borders. He furnishes by my count five major reasons for recommending this counter-intuitive strategy.

1. In the 1967 or "Six Day War", Friedman asserts that "the 1949 borders actually gave Israel a strategic advantage," namely, the ability to fight from "relatively compact terrain," which facilitated coordination, "timing and intensity of combat to suit their capabilities." Israel may have "lacked strategic depth, but it made up for it with compact space and interior lines."

2. Greater land area means "expanding the scope of the battlefield" and this in turn multiples "opportunities for intelligence failure," increases the "rate of consumption of supplies" from its allies, and leads to a perilous dependence on the shifting political calculations of foreign powers.

3. Given the menace of both asymmetric and unconventional warfare, the shape of Israel's borders is moot anyway, since Israel would be no less exposed in its post-1967 borders than it already was in 1949.

4. By insisting on its current borders, Israel alienates its allies. The precise borders should be those that "do not create barriers to aid when that aid is most needed." The pre-1967 borders provide Israel with a better chance "of maintaining critical alliances" and would also require "a smaller industrial base" for the production of weaponry, thus reducing dependence of foreign supply chains.

5. Generally speaking, "perpetual occupation would seem to place Israel at a perpetual disadvantage."

Friedman then concludes that Israel must "restructure its geography along the more favorable lines that existed between 1949 and 1967," when the country was "unambiguously victorious in its wars, rather than the borders and policies after 1967, when Israel has been less successful."

Let us examine each of these points in turn.

1. In an age of advanced weaponry, rapid military strikes, and blanket rocket fire, especially in more densely populated regions, a smaller Israel is an increasingly vulnerable Israel. A "relatively compact terrain" is a killing field in the making.

2. "Intelligence failure" is always possible irrespective of the size of the battlefield. Foreign chanceries and military headquarters where decisions are made remain where they are in enemy territory and do not necessarily expand or contract to coincide with the borders of the nation at risk. *The real question is whether good intelligence, once gathered, can be acted on.* For example, American intelligence was aware that the 9/11 attack was brewing, but failed to coordinate its various departments and resources to thwart the impending catastrophe. Moreover, foresight and exigent stockpiling and

preparation can overcome foreign dependence in anything but a war of attrition, which is not the nature of the sudden eruptions between Israel and its antagonists.

3. A strong perimeter, such as a state-of-the-art security fence, and unflagging vigilance can frustrate asymmetric warfare, as has already been shown. As for an unconventional or CBRN attack (Chemical, Biological, Radiological, Nuclear), this is a menace all nations are subject to regardless of land area. At the same time, a more substantial hinterland with forward monitoring sites permits better detection capabilities, since even a matter of minutes can be decisive, and gives the urban heartland the shield of additional distance.

4. Israel's "allies" have always proven to be fickle and unreliable, whether we are considering Eisenhower's self-admitted mistake in intervening in the 1956 Egyptian campaign or France's betrayal of Israel or the UNIFIL forces in Lebanon permitting Hezbollah to re-arm in violation of UN Resolution 1701 or President Obama's agenda to render Israel increasingly defenseless against its terrorist enemies. Israel cannot depend on the good faith or treaty obligations of its allies whatever its geographical dimensions.

5. The phrase "perpetual occupation" is a misnomer and an oft-repeated blue lobster mantra. Israel withdrew from its buffer zone in South Lebanon and was rewarded with an Iranian-supplied missile armada trained on its cities. Israel withdrew from Gaza and reaped thousands of Hamas rockets falling on its civilian centers. The Palestinian Authority controls almost the entirety of the West Bank. There is no "occupation" in the present acceptation of the term, but mainly "facts on the ground" entailing some scattered hamlets in the Shomron, the inevitable population growth in the vicinity of Jerusalem and the necessary security apparatus to prevent the infiltration of suicide bombers.

Friedman's conclusion is, in consequence, largely untenable. The reason Israel did *comparatively* poorly in its post-1967 wars has little or nothing to do with its expanded boundaries or the supposed onset of macromania. Rather we must look to the inescapable human frailties of over-confidence and complacency, the conviction that past successes augur future victories, which leads to the subliminal assumption of invincibility. The prelude to the 1973 or "Yom Kippur War," in which Israel was effectively asleep at the wheel, is an illustration of this predictable weakness and lapse of judgment. The somewhat disheveled condition of the army during the 2006 Summer War is another such instance. Yet another enfeebling element is — or was — the pervasive feeling of weariness after two generations of unrelenting conflict, expressed by former Prime Minister Ehud Olmert in his infamous "we are tired of winning" speech.

No less significant, programmatic left-wing defeatism and utopian irreality in the press and the academy plainly had a role to play in arranging for the country's more recent miseries. The deterioration in the quality of the Israeli leadership was also a salient factor in the country's suffering — a Barak who fled Lebanon in the night, a Sharon who went back on his word in disengaging from Gaza, an Olmert and a Livni ready to give up the store to their Palestinian "peace partners." Blue lobsters all, these leaders-in-name-only were all willing to comply with their so-called "allies" and to recede, as per Friedman and others, to smaller, less defensible or protected borders. In doing so, they brought only various forms of burden and distress to their people.

Clearly, the extension of Israel's border is completely irrelevant to its malaise, notwithstanding what our "experts" seem to think. What we are remarking here is not responsible tradecraft but a kind of mental aberration at work. More and more, we are led and lectured to by people who are prone to delusions of self-importance coupled with magical thinking, the belief that an ideological slogan, noble intentions, an unsupported theory or a wave of the negotiating wand can accomplish results that only humility, insight, practical acumen and a dedication to long-haul survival can yield. All Western nations have succumbed to this deformity of thought, but tiny Israel in its territorial corset is most in jeopardy.

Public intellectuals and political leaders are the bizarre crustaceans of our time.

Unfortunately, the blue lobsters of the political and ideological domain tend to proliferate and reproduce with abandon. They swim not only in the waters off Prince Edward Island but in all the oceans of the world. Armored against the lessons of reality and convinced of their uniqueness, they glitter in the media and international forums, oblivious to their natal incongruity. Whether we are considering public intellectuals like Friedman, whose numbers are legion, or political authorities who have allowed themselves to be swayed by fantasies of sophistication, they are not so much genetic anomalies as intellectual misfits, political incompetents and, what is most disheartening, a pod of eccentrics who threaten to become the norm.

The Divine Frenzy of Feminism

If the spirit of the classical Greek playwright Euripides could be summoned from the grave and observe our feminist age, he would not be surprised. In *The Bacchae* (premiered *circa* 405 B.C.), he told the story of Pentheus, the unfortunate ruler of Thebes, who resisted the ritual incursion of Dionysus, the androgynous god of wine, ecstasy, passionate delirium, and the oracular Mysteries.

In the play, Dionysus returns to Thebes, the city of his birth, accompanied by a retinue of bacchants, or drunken revellers. Finding himself mocked, he infects the women of the royal household with an excess of divine frenzy, whereupon they flee into the forest to perform paroxysms of fevered worship. Pentheus wishes to preserve the functioning of the state and recognizes that the upsurge of visionary dementia and phobic irrationality exemplified by the maenads or "raving ones"—the RadFem hordes of the day—would lead to the disruption of the political order and the destabilization of civil society.

Pentheus intends to put an end to the insanity but, influenced by Dionysus, falls prey to curiosity and is persuaded to disguise himself in women's clothing, enter the forest and witness the maenadic revels from a perch in a tall fir tree. He is spotted by the tribe of hysterics, brought to the ground and ripped to shreds, the mordancy of the scene enhanced by the fact that it is his own mother, Agave, who tears off his head and carries the trophy back to Thebes.

Of course, the play is far more complex than this short synopsis would indicate. Euripides treats the perennial conflict between the Olympian gods and the maternal Furies, between man and woman, between social order and individual enthusiasm, between Apollo, the god of reason and light, and Dionysus representing the darker forces of emotion and rapture—or as we would say today, of libido.

This theme was famously addressed by Euripides' great predecessor Aeschylus in the *Oresteian Trilogy*, where the female goddesses the *Eumenides* (or Furies) are pitted against the male Olympians. Both forces, Aeschylus felt, the visceral and the rational, were necessary to the proper conduct of the state and in the life of the individual, but must be contained in a condition of approximate balance to avoid a descent into anarchy. The message of *The Bacchae*, however, is ambiguous insofar as the conclusion of the play suggests the desired victory of the Dionysian infatuation, yet the disintegration of public order and Apollonian statecraft would have been obvious to Euripides' audience. We recall that Plato's *Republic*, in which music, art, and trance-like phenomena were to be the prohibited by law, appeared *circa* 380 B.C., only 25 years after the initial performance of *The Bacchae*. Both sides of the dynamic had their dedicated votaries.

Perhaps it was ever thus as one or another of these indispensable forces inevitably comes to predominate. Indeed, the Greek tragedians seemed to understand that the battle between male structure and female sentiment was an eternal fact of human life. For Aeschylus, to privilege one over the other ends in disaster—"Either way, ruin," as Agamemnon laments in the first play of the Trilogy, a phrase adopted by the philosopher G.W.F. Hegel in his *Lectures on Aesthetics* as a capsule definition of tragedy. For Euripides, the labile spirit of the feminine must be released into the world, whatever the cost. Yet, despite the priority given to Dionysus and his "agenda," there are, as it were, strong premonitory elements in *The Bacchae* that apply to our contemporary dilemma in which carceral feminism has come to cultural prominence.

In the current historical moment, the trance afflicting our radical feminists is not imposed from without, as in the play, but is self-induced, leading to a nationwide vendetta against so-called "toxic masculinity." The belief that the "patriarchy" is responsible for all of society's ills has produced destructive consequences: the ubiquitous allegations targeting men for sexual misconduct on the flimsiest of pretexts, the reduction of normative sexuality to the status of an aberration or a crime, the shunting of jurisprudence away from the English Common Law principle of "burden of proof" toward the dodgy concept of "preponderance of evidence" (i.e., whatever the adjudicator *feels* is likely or credible, almost always in favor of the female plaintiff), the campaign to Ritalin young male students into a state of narcolepsy, the precipitous decline of male university graduates, and the accelerating collapse of the institution of marriage. Contemporary feminists are Euripidean maenads in modern form, metaphorically and, in social effect, tearing men limb from limb in a fury of pathogenic derangement.

What is also interesting is that Pentheus allows himself to be persuaded to wear female attire in order to carry out his reconnaissance unobserved. *Mutatis mutandis,* a version of his regrettable decision is currently flourishing among us as men come increasingly to side with the feminist prepossession—judges, teachers, political leaders, university administrators, intellectuals, talking heads supporting the feminist dogma that women are society's innocent victims and men violent oppressors and ruthless demagogues who must be denounced, punished, brought low like Pentheus from his tree, and ultimately feminized.

Men now find themselves in a binary Penthean condition: on the one hand, the profusion of beta males sporting their inner maenadic vestments—aka manginas and "white knights," emanations of the god whose epithets include *Dionysos Dimorphos* (dual-formed), *gunnis* (womanish man), and *pseudanor* (counterfeit man); and on the other, men who wish to remain men being culturally dismembered and socially castrated. The balance between the sexes, both biological and cultural, is now communally distorted beyond recognition as Dionysus celebrates his triumph over Apollo and the Furies swarm Mount Olympus.

"It is precisely Dionysus' identification with the feminine," writes classical scholar Froma Zeitlin in *Sexuality and Gender in the Classical*

World, that allows the god to introduce "confusions, conflicts, tensions and ambiguities" into the hierarchical masculine world, thus disrupting "the normal social categories" and impairing male confidence and authority to the detriment of the whole. This is where we have arrived in our era of Dionysian madness.

As Agave laments at the end of *The Bacchae*, "It was Dionysus who proved our ruin; now I see it all." In demanding obeisance to temperamental fury at the expense of the principle of order, feminists and their allies have unleashed a storm of discontent, resentment, misrule, and social turmoil whose consequences will be catastrophic. Without the reassertion of proud and inherent masculinity to restore the equilibrium between the sexes, the road to political suicide and cultural decay is wide open and we will all, women as well as men, suffer for it.

Politics and Music

"Politics is for old men." Thus a Serbian friend informed me when I visited Belgrade shortly before everything fell apart. He wanted me to send him Beatles albums not easily obtainable at the time so he could listen to "happy music," by which he meant just music. Unfortunately, politics is for young men (and women) too, and although good music uncorrupted by politics can still be found, bad music with a political or subversive agenda abounds.

As Michael Walsh argues in his magisterial *The Devil's Pleasure Palace*, "we must see music and art as separate and apart from politics, no matter the quotidian circumstances that give them birth." Certainly, aside from military marches and national anthems, music is for the most part not the right medium for political feelings, commentary and themes—except indirectly, as in Country and Western, when the singer expresses his or her love of country or commitment to traditional ways of life.

Far too much music exists to peddle a political or disruptive message, often a predictably leftist screed. Historian Victor Davis Hanson ruefully states in an essay titled *Epitaph for a Dying Culture* that many people now skip popular music "on the expectation that it is not just vulgar and foul, but incoherently politicalized." As I pointed out in an earlier article for *American Thinker*, typical examples are furnished by such truly execrable groups as Rage Against the Machine, the violence-prone deathcore Slipknot (whose fans are known as "maggots"), the ludicrously named Prophets of Rage, the ostentatiously punky Red Hot Chili Peppers, along with Vampire Weekend and Foster the People shilling for socialist hack Bernie Sanders, the manically feminist co-ed War On Women advancing its new wave feminism agenda, and the hardcore rocker band Stick To Your Guns, the latter dedicating their piece of cacophonic rubbish "What Choice Did You Give Us" to the families of hooligans like Eric Garner, Mike Brown and Trayvon Martin.

Let's not forget the wildly popular Maroon V. Featured on the 2019 Super Bowl halftime show, Maroon V is a band characterized by wretched lyrics ("yeah" and "uh" and "oooh" are notable phatics), hackneyed semi-melodies, lots of tats, feminist bona fides and refugee-friendly sentiment—"Liberation not Deportation" is lead singer Adam Levine's printed mantra. The videos of their hit song "Girls Like You" foreground socially prominent women wearing T-shirts festooned with identity group and "social justice" slogans. That lesbian Ellen DeGeneres and radical Muslima Ilhan Omar are among the dippy terpsichoreans is not unexpected. The result is laughable, especially DeGeneres hopping up and down like an animated pogo stick. There can be little doubt that what we are observing is PC motivated musical trash.

These are all instances of music gone rancid with political advocacy, almost always of the jejune leftist stamp. Unsurprisingly, many of these rockers and folkers become social justice warriors, peace ambassadors, philanthropic missionaries and rabid environmentalists—without, however, studying the real science or manifold complexities behind the causes they embrace. Like Hollywood entertainers and many national politicians, they are not remarkable for intelligence.

Neil Young's well-known bloviations on social justice and environmental issues fall into the same bottomless pit of popular claptrap. Ditto Bono, whose well-publicized charity work has done more for Bono than for the world's poor. As *Rolling Stone* informs us, Bono "became a major business mogul, cofounding Elevation Partners to invest in entertainment and media businesses, one being the Forbes Media group, another being a company that makes war-simulation video games." One thinks, too, of Cat Stevens whose conversion to the "religion of peace" as Yusuf Islam did not prevent him from calling for the death of Salman Rushdie for writing the dazzling and hilarious *The Satanic Verses*.

Billy Joe Armstrong, lead singer of Green Day, approved of North Korea's mad dictator Kim Jong-un over his own president, Donald Trump. The antisemitic bigot Roger Waters, of Pink Floyd fame, embarked on a vendetta against Israel, the only democratic state in the Middle East quagmire. Another case in point is rapper Eminem whose neuroleptic lyrics coupled with his intellectual vacancy render both his music and his politics fatuously pubescent. He is now vying for attention by dissing Donald Trump while mangling the English language.

Indeed, the farrago of sanctimonious juvenilia that disguises itself as music, from metal to protopunk to grunge and glam, often affecting to be socially conscious, is an affront to both common sense and musical sense. As for what we call "rave music"—acid, techno, trance, liquid funk and other subgenres—it is not really music at all but a kind of jungle orgiastic or lupercalian debauch meant to stimulate a kinesthetic reaction.

The same is true of rap, the vulgarity and infantile babbling of which are symptoms of an increasingly degenerate culture. A form of social and political protest against the perceived racial disparities embedded in the culture, it is certainly not music. Its lyrics are obscene bordering on depraved and its melodic structure is non-existent, though it exhibits a rant-and-chant primal cadence. It is, in effect, one of the militant wings of leftist political culture whose purpose is the destabilization of traditional mores.

Some might claim that the anti-establishment protest songs of the Sixties (Bob Dylan, Joan Baez, Phil Ochs, etc.) demonstrate that politics and music can indeed go together, but I would contend that the lyrics of most of these songs are mortifyingly insipid and ideologically faddish. Moreover, though they may once have been effective as political statement, they tend to be musically ephemeral—who hums them now? The one exception to the rule I can think of is Pete Seeger, a bore as an advocate for partisan causes but co-composer of some lovely and memorable songs ("Where Have All the Flowers Gone?," "If I Had a Hammer").

The Canadian group GY!BE (Godspeed You! Black Emperor), like its American and German screamo counterparts, is a purveyor of ostentatiously bad music that relies on special effects like mind-numbing decibels, near total darkness and garishly spotlit films. As spokesmen for the power chord genre, the troupe argues that "All music is political, right? You either make music that pleases the king and his court, or you make music for the serfs outside the walls… It's what music is for, right?" Wrong. They go on to assert that the function of music is "to distract or confront, or both at the same time." Wrong again.

One thinks of Dixie Chick Natalie Maine's comment to *Rolling Stone*: "We always felt like we were searching for ways to make an impact outside of music." The band's denunciation of President Bush for apparently shaming Texas, their rejection of patriotism, their feminist avowals in "Sin Wagon" ("Feel like Delilah lookin' for a Samson") and "Goodbye Earl" (it's OK to kill an abusive husband—nothing about abusive wives and false accusations) are disturbing. They display what feminist musicologist Susan McClary in *Feminist Endings* extols as gendered feelings in musical productions and discourse. Yet one of the band's most influential backers was the disgraced Harvey Weinstein. Aside from beat and rhythm and the fact that they are an all-girl band (albeit with male back-up), the songs in themselves are not particularly memorable or distinctive.

Music must remain vigilant. The drivel of much contemporary popular music has surrendered character, melody and memorability in the service of dubious political and "social justice" objectives. When music turns to propaganda, solicitation, apology or imprecation rather than joy, celebration, reflection or even melancholy, it has lost its soul.

I am tempted to make an exception for Billy Cool and his fledgling band '55MAGAton, which Mark Ellis describes as "heavy-ish rock and roll, with a southern flavor" and Billy depicts as "satiric [and] pro-Trump." Judging from the videos, he is talented and witty, as well as politically savvy. "The obvious potential hazard," he notes, "is the radical left…It's a shame that the current political climate essentially limits free speech." Intelligent satire, amusing lyrics and capable musicianship go some way to countenancing political content, but the horizon is narrow and the prospects generally ephemeral. (Another exception involves the parodic genius of Tom Lehrer, but his satire, as funny as it was controversial, cast a wide net, dealing with a plethora of topical subjects. For all its brilliance, it remains a niche phenomenon, and not to my purpose here.)

Plato banished music from his oligarchic Republic for corrupting the youth, a classical fatwa seconded by Iran's Ayatollah Khomeini who abolished music from his Republic as encouraging frivolity and stupefaction. The equally totalitarian left has not so much expunged music from the polity as debased it almost past recognition, precisely for the purpose of promoting stupefaction. But the intention remains the same, the creation on the one hand of an indoctrinated and docile populace and, on the other, of a cadre of doctrinal guerillas. Good music in any genre opens the mind and speaks to the heart. Political music, promoting the memes and shibboleths of the era, whether of fascist or communist or anarchistic orientation, closes the mind and stultifies the heart. In most music of this nature the message is heavy and the sentiment is trite. It may make for interesting theatre, but not much of lasting good can come of it.

The trouble is multiple—the singer, the song and the infatuated audience—but anyone who wishes to make truly beautiful music must come by it honestly regardless of its reception, indifferent to the fashions and fetishes of the day and free of chronic self-obsession—at least in the moment of composition. Renouncing what has become an amalgam of narcissism and sanctimoniousness, the maker of songs must speak to what is permanent in the human heart and soul. *Caveat cantor.*

The University Is Ripe for Replacement

The Academy is now enemy-occupied territory. Beginning in early K-12 and continuing to the highest levels of university education, Leftist indoctrination is the gravest dilemma that afflicts education in North America, rendering it perhaps the most powerful instrument of anti-Western bias and socialist propaganda of the modern era.

Here my concern is with the abandonment of genuine scholarship, fact-based historical research, familiarity with the "Great Books" and the development of critical thinking habits, particularly in the Humanities and Social Sciences. The curriculum now in place is one of intellectual dysphoria promoting the circulation of false or unprovable narratives—Anthropogenic Global Warming, Islam as a religion of peace, the campus rape epidemic, toxic masculinity, the scandal of American history, the glories of "diversity and inclusion," the benefits of Socialism, to cite just a few among a veritable encyclopedia—and furthering the revolutionary project of social and political deconstruction. Education has been transformed into a grooming operation for social justice warriors, radical feminists, anti-white vigilantes and budding socialists.

Moreover, to compound the septic plunge into calamitous absurdity, the self-contradictory adoption of a kind of state religion of postmodern thought and doctrine—briefly, the suspicion of reason, the belief that reality is a conceptual construct, the rejection of fixed or objective truth—has served to turn the university into a parody of its original purpose, the pursuit of genuine knowledge.

Defenders of the status quo need to be taken not with a grain of salt but an entire salt mine. Case in point: *Globe and Mail* columnist Doug

Saunders, a rabid anti-conservative, an apologist for Islam, a believer in rampant immigration, and one of the shoddiest journalists in Canada, fully rejects the charge of university malfeasance. Rather, he claims, the campus is "less radical, more tolerant, more open and more politically moderate than ever before."

The fantasy bubble that bullhorns like Saunders inhabit seems pretty well impermeable. You cannot reason with people who are immune to facts or, for whatever reason, consider countervailing evidence an offense against subjective conviction. They are either useful idiots or handy liars. Better to attend to an acclaimed historian like Niall Ferguson who, in an interview on the *Dave Rubin Report*, pointed out that since the late Sixties and early Seventies, the Left has been busy replicating itself in the universities via targeted recruiting, to the extent that today "90% plus of faculty members are liberals or progressivists, if not outright Marxists."

As H.G Wells said in a fawning 1934 interview with Josef Stalin, "There can be no revolution without a radical change in the educational system." To which Stalin replied, "That is a correct observation." The "radical change," of course, is socialism, which a craven administration and a squalid faculty are assiduously promoting.

Innumerable authoritative books have been published and evidence-based articles posted on the corruption and virtual death of the university as an institution of higher learning, which interested readers can find with a click on the keyboard. Robert Nisbet's 1971 *The Degradation of Academic Dogma* is a classic in the field. The more the university became a self-governing corporation, he wrote, "the less noble it proved to be in both purpose and bearing," that is, in failing to concentrate on the pursuit of knowledge and the preservation its ancestral dignity. As a "community of mind," it has surrendered to "its own hubris."

Warren Treadgold's recently released *The University We Need* expands the argument, taking on the postmodern heresy that itself would have been sufficient to ruin education in the West. Given the university's obsession with the paradigm of oppressors and oppressed, Treadgold writes, "Postmodernism meant that all contrary facts could be dismissed as attempts to enforce oppression…The creations of leftist scholarship included the elements of 'multiculturalism'…such as a feminist Africa, a pacifist Islam, and an evil United States and Western Europe." His castigation of the curricular and programmatic direction the university has taken is irrefutably damning.

Treadgold, however, believes that the university can be reformed, and this is where we part company. Be it said, his recommendations are sensible, such as reducing university funding to a 20% budgetary limit and advocating for new and responsible leadership that would eschew mediocre ideas, books, students and professors. He concludes by stating: "If someone has better ideas for improving [the academy] than judging professors by the quality of their work or founding a new university dedicated to excellence, the time to share those ideas is now." I suspect, though, that Treadgold's "new university" is the present university rehabilitated and restored to its former glory. And the present university is not going away any time soon.

I agree that government funding should be selectively but drastically reduced—and strict oversight procedures predicated on standards of disciplinary excellence and free inquiry set in place—in order to render these *de facto* industries rational and culturally competitive. A parasitical administration should be lopped in half. The burgeoning numbers of noxious "diversity and inclusion" officers should be summarily dismissed, preferably without pensions. They have done enough damage. As in Hungary, Gender Studies departments need to be shuttered as non-scholarly and doctrinaire induction centers for social inadequates. Unqualified university applicants, regardless of politics, race, gender, creed or ethnicity, should not be admitted: all students should be judged solely on merit and desert, irrespective of parenthetical concerns. It should be acknowledged that Social Justice is not in the academic purview: truth and scholarship are its reason for being. Justice is the court's domain.

But these are optative proposals. The chances that they will actually be put into cumulative effect strike me as bordering on zero. We should also consider that efforts to reform the university might only contribute to its endurance. It may conceivably permit a few reforms as a sop to its adversaries, but the situation will persist. After all, the universities are no longer knowledge guilds, but self-regulating commercial and doctrinaire systems interested primarily in profit and social revisionism. They will double down to preserve their turf. The Academy is now enemy-occupied territory, defended by a formidable army of the ignorant, the corrupt, the vulgar and the perverse, and they are not about to surrender their sinecures.

It may be preferable for real scholars and concerned parties to begin planning for a parallel university structure, whether as online sites or physical plants or both. In the words of *American Thinker* editor Thomas Lifson, "fundamental change of the institutional map is necessary." (Personal correspondence.) One can begin with Treadgold's recommendations as applied to a *fresh and separate institution* embodying the measures proposed above, while seeking funding from alumni disenchanted with their alma maters, conservative organizations, crowd-sourcing, and a pragmatic and far-sighted government like the one presently in power in the United States. Culture-hero Jordan Peterson is already busy designing an online university to supplant the current "indoctrination cults." There are bugs still to be worked out, but the process is underway. Start small, think big.

Insuperable as the task may seem, perhaps something truly new will emerge on which, with patience, experience and foresight, we can build. In a time of civilizational decline, a wholly new university may serve to prolong our historical tenure. The key is to resist despair, strategize effectively, remain prepared and remember the principles of moral reason and intellectual excellence on which restitution depends. The modern university is a moribund institution and cannot be reformed. It is ripe for replacement.

The Shaping of Our Destiny

A nation whose leaders, whose cultural elite, and a moiety of whose people have given themselves over to every conceivable form of decadence has been demonstrably faltering, its greatness receding into the past. It is a nation that slaughters its unborn in an orgy of indifferent cruelty, giving offerings to Moloch; that mercilessly extorts the living substance from those of its citizens who still struggle toward decency and the values of community; that sets bread and circuses over justice; that has invested its energies in raising a Tower of Babel rather than a Temple of Gratefulness; that has eviscerated the language and enervated thought under the sign of political correctness; that launches a virulent campaign against the Christian system of values which, as David Horowitz eloquently argues in his recent *Dark Agenda*, is at the root of American democracy; and that pays no heed to the noble intentions of its Founding Fathers. In his aptly titled book *Coming Apart*, Charles Murray concludes that "the American project is disintegrating." The four domains of happiness he identifies — family, vocation, community, and faith — "have all been enfeebled."

Is this plunge into the abyss of corruption and venality merely a function of historical inevitability — all things human, great and small, must eventually decline? Or is a devastating punishment being levied on a nation that has sold its soul, that has lost its way, that refuses to recognize an authority superior to itself and has sunk into a morass of pervasive immorality? What reasonable person cannot be troubled by the spectacle of shallowness, self-aggrandizement, utter ignorance, and sanctioned immorality that confronts and embraces us? These sound like quaint notions that can appeal only to the naïve and the zealots. And yet what conscientious person can say with absolute assurance that such is not the case?

Broadly speaking, these two explanations for cultural, national, and civilizational decline—the evolutionary-historical and the moral-theological—are similar in the effects they postulate, but they differ insofar as the latter allows for the tempering of justice with mercy—that is, for the mollification of a just if vengeful deity. The reversal of decline, a stay of execution, remains possible, assuming a people rethinks itself at the eleventh hour, repudiating its penchant for pandemic depravity, and seeks to restore a lost courage, honor, humility, and fundamental decency in its national life. The downward path is effortless, a law of cultural gravity; the upward path is arduous and against the national grain but theoretically possible. In secular terms, following the upward path is called wisdom or prudence; in religious terms, it is known as grace or salvation, the gift of divine concern. True, Abraham may have lost his bargain, but God was willing to listen. And perhaps still is.

It is always tempting for those of a certain cast of mind to discern the hand of God operating in human affairs. "There's a divinity that shapes our ends / Rough-hew them how we will," says Hamlet. If an eminent thinker like Adam Smith can propose an "invisible hand" operating in the economic realm, why cannot a brilliant theologian like Karl Barth affirm that "the best proof of God's existence is the existence of the Jewish people"? Can we not say the same of the improbable ascent and unique political character of the American republic in the history of the world? Perhaps the two domains of the empirical and the spiritual are not as distinct as we have been led to believe. May not the election of Donald Trump—a flawed man serving a higher cause—coupled with the defeat of the most corrupt and vindictive political figure in the country, represent the intervention of the numinous in the life of a once-great nation that can be made great again? Who can say?

The questions we now face are crucial. Has America truly changed course at the pivotal moment, whether by sheer accident or transcendent guidance? Will it last? The Edomites are still swarming, and the rift between that part of the nation committed to the values of work, family, and creative expenditure and that part of the nation mired in ignorance, pride, and destructive sentimentality—in effect, between heartland and coast, rural and urban, fly-over and touch-down, conservative and left-liberal — appears to be permanent.

Questions persist. Will Trump revise his stated principles for national recovery and accede to some of his opponents' policies and demands? Will the Electoral College one day "flip" or be abolished, allowing a "social justice" bigot to eke out a marginal victory? Will the Democrats finally impose the one-party despotism they seek? The devil always finds a way to work his mischief; alternatively, Edgar Allan Poe's "imp of the perverse" abides perpetually in the human soul.

The hope is that the best part of the nation can survive the burden of its parasites and drones and still manage to prosper. Yuval Levin in *The Fractured Republic* sees America as essentially a "creedal nation" animated by "a love of the ideal that we have always held out before ourselves as the American possibility…put forward in the Declaration of Independence," a nation "built up out of communities." Similarly, James Pierson in *Shattered Consensus*, though agreeing with Charles Murray that America is in "a process of unravelling," remains hopeful of a future trajectory opening the way "for a new chapter in the unfolding history of the American idea."

Considering the totally implausible result of the 2016 election, and assuming that the worrisome events mentioned above fail to materialize, may we not suggest that there are a sufficient number of the just and deserving, a saving remnant, for a "new chapter" to be opened in the history of the republic, or to put it another way, for the Abrahamic bargain to be won? Is there more to the election of Donald Trump than meets the skeptical eye?

Mere speculation, of course.

The Canadian Temper: A Warning to America

Canadians have long thought of themselves as morally superior to supposedly vulgar and abrasive Americans. According to the self-justifying Canadian mythos, we embody a more enlightened and humane outlook on the world. In addition to oil, maple syrup, and lumber, our most valuable export—our gift, we imagine, to our southern neighbors—is our vision of a sustainable and irenic future. Let us examine the most current incarnation of that vision.

Canada is essentially a socialist country, closer to the increasingly decrepit European welfare and statist paradigm than to the (now faltering) classic American model of individual self-reliance. Canada instituted social programs like state-funded medicine relying on major tax hikes long before it became an issue in the U.S., and gambled on multiculturalism as a viable national project, in effect, as a kind of political eschatology. There is no question that the Canadian temper has always been more politically Arcadian than the American.

The current refugee question in particular has become a pivotal and collective expression of this temper, with citizens opening their wallets, hearts and homes to a migratory influx from the Islamic world. Our self-congratulatory generosity is amply demonstrated in the writings of celebrated Constitutional lawyer Julius Grey. Pontificating in the *Montreal Gazette*, Grey urges the welcoming of thousands of Syrian migrants as we proceed "to create a society which has, on the one hand, citizens of myriad origins and, on the other, no barriers between them."

The problem that Grey refused to confront or even identify is that immigrants and refugees from historically backward, theocratic, anti-Semitic, Sharia-dominated and terror-sponsoring nations are precisely the ones who are creating "barriers," such as purpose-built ghettos, no-go zones, closed neighborhoods, special privileges and spaces, an atmosphere of threat, and who have no interest in Western-style "individual autonomy and freedom"—Grey's chosen vocabulary. Grey is the lawyer for the Muslim-friendly socialist New Democratic Party, but there is not much sunlight between the NDP and the governing Muslim-friendly Liberal Party.

Indeed, in the October 2015 Federal election the Liberals, the NDP and the splinter, reactionary-left Greens ran between them a total of 23 Muslim candidates (the leftist/sovereignist *Bloc Québécois* fielded two Muslim candidates, raising the combined total to 25 Muslim hopefuls), representing approximately 7 per cent of available parliamentary seats, over twice the Islamic percentage of the population. (The ousted Conservatives fielded only four Muslims.) In the end, the combined electoral seats won by the four left-leaning parties, the Liberals, NDP, *Bloc* and Greens, clocked in at 71 per cent; the center-right Conservatives polled just 29 per cent. *This* is the face of Canada today.

During the election campaign, Islam became a prominent issue, with Liberal PM Justin Trudeau claiming that there was no place in his Canada for the previous Conservative government's "divisive" Islamophobia and exaggerated concern for national security. In his victory speech, Trudeau uttered the inevitable pieties à la Obama: "We beat fear with hope, we beat cynicism with hard work. We beat negative, divisive politics with a positive vision that brings Canadians together." To a Muslim woman wearing a hijab, he promised "a government that believes deeply in the diversity of this country."

A perverse illustration of this stupefying attitude comes from the Bank of Nova Scotia (commonly known as Scotiabank), which has welcomed the migrant onslaught with its Welcome Syrians program. (The original webpage featuring large print and colorful graphics now seems to have been scrubbed.) Canada's third largest bank offered every "Syrian" a hundred dollar gift deposit, a $2000 limit unsecured credit card, a free safety deposit box for one year and a $50 unsecured overdraft. Customers who bank at the Scotia and pay monthly fees to maintain their accounts had good reason to feel resentful—unless, of course, they happen to be migrant sympathizers and soft on Islam.

These "Syrians," not all of whom are Syrians and some of whom are almost surely ISIS jihadists, receive housing, benefits and gifts without having contributed an iota to the nation's economy; indeed, they will be a limitless drain on our resources.

The $1.2 billion cost of bringing in these refugees is only the beginning of our fiscal woes. Quoted by the CBC, coordinator Carl Nicholson said "many factors have made the task of housing government-assisted refugees more difficult, including the larger-than expected size of some families that have arrived." The accompanying photo shows a couple with six toddlers. No wonder the Liberals' shopworn immigration minister (now resigned) John McCallum solicited the business community for donations in the amount of $50 million. "I would encourage all Canadians, companies, individuals, communities, to continue to support the effort because we are entering a critical phase," he said. Darn right on the latter score.

My parents and grandparents, fleeing starving, war-torn Ukraine, worked to the bone to earn a living while contributing through taxes to the national welfare. Many Canadians share the same history, yet they are expected to receive and bankroll a large number of migrants who will take advantage of the innumerable perks that our forebears, who fled famine and civil war and who helped build this country, had never enjoyed or even considered their due.

Richard Butrick cogently argues in an important article for *American Thinker* that immigrants who came to America in the 19th and early 20th centuries "knew they had to work hard to survive," at the same time contributing to the nation's commercial, industrial and scientific advances. "Immigrants today," he continues, "know the U.S. is a fail-safe environment," where they are subsidized and coddled. The so-called "re-energizing" immigration narrative has been superseded by, let's say, a parasitical model based on muddled sentimentality and false calculations, which Canada has bought into without sober forethought. A country built on welfare migrants is not a country built on hardworking immigrants.

There are some signs that the "Syrian Covenant" is becoming more complicated than originally envisaged, as the initial euphoria for the migrants seems to be waning under an unforgiving reality. I have heard that families that gloatingly affirmed their "Canadian values" and freely took "Syrians" into their homes are petitioning the government for financial help. The City of Ottawa, Canada's capital, has called for a pause to its hospitality for lack of housing, facilities and funds. Toronto, Vancouver and Halifax have also asked for a hiatus. The Radison Hotel in Toronto in which refugees have been housed has become uninhabitable to guests, rife with theft and swimming in filth. The bloom is starting to come off the rose—and the hue off the rose-colored glasses—for many of these fallow enthusiasts. But with further government subventions and the media propaganda blitz saturating what remains of the Canadian mind, the early stages of skepticism and reluctance will probably lead to nothing much.

This is how we do things in Canada. We throw out a Conservative government—itself an anomaly in our political landscape—that steered us safely through the devastating market crash of 2007/8 and objected to Islamic face coverings in citizenship swearing-in ceremonies and to the acceptance of "barbaric" practices in the cultural habits of these new citizens—and bring in a Liberal administration dedicated to increasing the national debt and gradually submerging the country in an effluvium of Muslim migrants and refugees.

The U.S. is clearly heading in the same direction with its national debt swelling exponentially and the inpouring of unvetted "Syrian" migrants exacerbating an already problematic Islamic infiltration. In effect, it's the same set of cultural attributes, a big spending mentality and an open door policy, of which Canada has long been a shining exemplar. This is one reason why the 2016 election was perhaps the most critical in U.S. history. A post-Obama Democrat administration under Billary or Bernie would have closed the gap between our two countries dramatically. And this is one reason (among many) why the election of Donald Trump may determine whether America can return to some degree of sanity and a semblance of its former vitality—or, heaven forfend, become Canada South.

The Perfect Algorithm

I find myself thinking quite a bit about algorithms these days. The word itself derives from the Latinized name of the Persian scholar Mohammed ibn-Musa al-Khwarizmi, reputedly the inventor of algebra, who flourished during the Abbasid Caliphate in ninth-century Baghdad. 1200 years later with the advent of the computer, the age of programming and machine-learning dawned, refining and applying al-Kwarizmi's scheme of numeration into conceptual regions he could never have imagined. According to the standard definition, an algorithm is a set of rules determining the nature and order of computer calculations, the major component of search engines that canvass data bases cued by key words.

In *The Master Algorithm*, Pedro Domingos writes: "A programmer—someone who creates algorithms and codes them up—is a minor god, creating universes at will. You could even say that the God of Genesis himself is a programmer." The serpent in Algorithm Eden is complexity—of space, time and human limitation—creating a world that grows "increasingly fragile." Data is turned into information and information is transformed into knowledge.

But the situation grows increasingly tangled when we realize that algorithms can reflect a programmer's ignorance or prejudice or explicit design, and that algorithms can also learn to rewrite themselves, that is, they can also be self-programming, introducing a degree of uncertainty into the original parameters. Knowledge may be skewed, infected by error, and even prey to delusions—a tree whose fruit should not be plucked and eaten.

Similarly, Frank Pasquale in *The Black Box Society* alerts us to the troubling fact that algorithms, often opaque to their own programmers, can serve to reinforce social taboos, prejudices and prior assumptions which reflect the unconscious attitudes of the programmers. But these attitudes may also be quite conscious, introducing a propagandistic element into the algorithm. Pasquale writes: "The proprietary algorithms... are immune from scrutiny," rendering us vulnerable to surveillance, censorship, and coercion masking as persuasion, and so "undermining the openness of our society." He points out that mining data from social media in the hunt for potential malefactors "comes with a high risk of false positives." We should be aware, too, that it comes with a growing certainty of false negatives. Indeed, given the monopolistic power of the major social media networks, practically all promoting progressivist memes and left-wing politics, such contamination is inevitable.

The principal social networks—Facebook, Google, Twitter, YouTube, Patreon, etc.—all rely on secret algorithms derived from human emotional and ideological input. As Jim Treacher writes at *PJ Media*, "Tech companies are notorious for their liberal culture. ... Worse, tech companies like Facebook, Google, Amazon, and Twitter have relied on the Southern Poverty Law Center (SPLC), a far-left smear factory that brands Conservative and Christian organizations 'hate groups.'" Clearly, these networks are not simply digital common carriers but a species of political cabal.

Niall Ferguson's study of network theory in *The Square and the Tower* shows us how we are often the victims of the "discrepancy between the ideal and reality," so that in "mak[ing] the world more connected"—Facebook's mission statement—these networks may actually have made the world more susceptible to manipulation. As noted, they filter out content deemed "hateful"—that is, unpalatable to the controllers, who routinely censor posts and messages of a conservative stripe on the excuse that they "look like spam" or constitute "hate speech"—and strive to foster "community governance" on a global scale, which is to say, mass control from the top down. In effect, these algorithmic conglomerates have become both the sign and the driver, as Ferguson says, of a world "falling apart."

The Perfect Algorithm

In my wackier moments, I like to fantasize that the confusion and thought-programming from which we suffer in the contemporary West is the product of a jihadist conspiracy, orchestrated by a Muslim mastermind named Mohammed al Gorithm, who has convinced us that Islam is a religion of peace and that those who object are guilty of Islamophobia. Or that a nefarious character whose real name is Al-Gorithm has managed to convince us that the globe is incinerating due to exponential carbon buildup. Of course, the databases relied upon here are subject to prior engineering, the information extracted is corrupted, and the knowledge acquired is filled with error about the world we live in.

On a more serious plane, we need to recognize that our beliefs and actions are increasingly predicated on falsehood. Islam is peaceful, the planet is growing warmer, the seas are rising and polar bears are on the verge of extinction. Ultimately, taking such calculations to their logical extreme, we can assert that gender is a social construction—there are 32 or more sexual morphisms with which we can identify—or that our universities are places of tolerance and free debate or that masculinity is toxic or that multicultural diversity makes us stronger or that socialism is the solution to all our political and economic problems. We create an alternate reality with no relation to actual social, political and physical reality which, to quote the philosopher Ludwig Wittgenstein in the *Tractatus Logico-Philosophicus*, is "all that is the case."

Rather, the algorithms currently operating in the social and political spheres have us chiefly believing and promoting all that is not the case. They have us behaving in ways that must infallibly lead to our demise as rational beings as we become human bots seeking an ever more fraudulent epistemology.

The German philosopher Hans Vaihinger, in his book *The Philosophy of 'As If'* (*Die Philosophie des Als Ob*), argued that "fictions" that are functionally serviceable, imaginary constructs that work and are "fruitful," may be regarded as true. Thus we might say there exists an algorithm unlike any of the others, a super algorithm that is, so to speak, plugged into the historical computer. Those who are programming us toward the abyss are not themselves responsible for the catastrophe that awaits. The progs, the feminists, the SJWs, the fetid creatures of the Swamp and the Deep State, a "liberation theologian" anti-pope, media moguls and university officials, billionaire socialists roiling the masses—they are merely elves and puppets, doing the bidding of the Master Programmer. They are the Great Manipulator's unwitting retainers, busy processing their culturally inspired subroutines that serve a supervening purpose, unaware they are involved in an eschatological mission.

Naturally, they are preoccupied by their own personal, local and temporal concerns, but it is "as if" they are themselves programmed by the super algorithm to bring the civilization of which they are a part to its terminal moment. They do not provide us with algorithms to live by, as Brian Christian and Tom Griffiths suggest in their book of that title, algorithms that "people can borrow for their own lives [to] better understand the errors that we make." These are algorithms to die by.

As for the Master Programmer whose super algorithm is ineluctable, none can say who or what it is, except to posit a quasi-mystical presence, one of whose names is Entropy, and whose algorithm governs the decline and death of civilizations like ours. Barring Divine intervention, there is no way around this algorithm. There is nothing we can do about it. The rules and commands are fixed. The ostensible villains delivering our ruin are merely its little helpers, nothing more.

Just as human beings are unavoidably prone to cellular programming, so civilizations are subject to the gradual silencing and shutting down of their historical trajectories. Their accounts are eventually blocked. I have no antidote to suggest that can frustrate the algorithmic teleology at work. All we can do is struggle episodically against the Master Programmer's baneful deputies, if only to defer the inevitable. It's better to go down tomorrow than today.

The Campus Rape Meme Just Keeps Chugging Along

College rape has become a national scandal. We are constantly informed that female students live in peril of being sexually assaulted in proportions that defy statistical credibility. Recently, for example, Andrea Horwath, Ontario NDP leader, claimed on national television that the university is a dangerous place since one in three female students will be sexually assaulted. No crime on the planet has such a victimization rate which, if true, would require something approaching martial law to redress. In any event, the NDP leader bravely confronted the danger visiting various campuses prior to the provincial elections. Andrea, however, judging from a recent appearance on CBC TV, is safe.

Thanks to such unseemly advocates and their emasculated brethren (who proliferate in the political, academic and legal professions from which their careers or ideological agendas materially advance), the rape meme has spread throughout the U.S. and Canada with bubonic rapidity. The real victims of the plague, however, are not female students but circumstantial evidence and common sense.

Let's consider. What responsible parent would send his or her daughter to university if she stood a 33% chance of being sexually assaulted and her life potentially ruined? Or would not labor to find an institution where she might conceivably emerge unscathed from her studies? And why, for that matter, would female students now outnumber their male counterparts by a significant number and graduate in greater numbers as well, which MIT economists David Autor and Melanie Wasserman in their 2013 study, *The Emerging Gender Gap in Labor Markets and Education*, call a "tectonic shift" in the educational landscape? The disparity is approximately 60-40 and, in some departments like English, as high as 80-20.

"[T]he gains of women have been nothing less than stunning," the MIT researchers observe. The same is true of various faculties, especially educational departments and medical school. Any objective and impartial study would reveal that women have done remarkably well while men have been psychologically raped and economically assaulted. No man is safe from unproven or anonymous allegations of sexual assault or from classroom prejudice, which explains the declining numbers of males attending and graduating university. Andrea Horwath is unintentionally right. The campus is indeed a dangerous place — not for women, but for men.

But facts cannot budge a meme. *USA Today* featured an article noting that 89% of colleges reported zero rapes in 2015. The author Patrick deHahn, however, is having none of it. After all, he argues, "*Reported* is really the key word. Just because a school had no rape reports doesn't mean no rapes happened." In a sense, deHahn is correct: "report" really is a key word, since his article is merely a "report" of a report, which, following the logic applied therein, does not mean that his report needs to be believed or accepted. Logic was never the strong suit for the radical feminist sorority and their male hangers-on, a cadre for whom the under-reporting of rape becomes indisputable proof that indiscriminate campus rape actually exists.

DeHahn then quotes another survey which reports, *pro forma*, that "more than one in five students said they experienced sexual abuse." Naturally, it is never made clear precisely what constitutes "sexual abuse." According to radical feminist Mary Koss, who helped start the accusatory rampage with her articles and books positing a one in four figure, almost anything can constitute sexual abuse: sexual comments, jokes, provocative remarks, verbal pressure.

In *The Rape Victim*, she enumerates "traumatic experiences" such as "unwanted touching," "non-consensual voyeurism," "workplace harassment," and "ostensibly consensual sexual intercourse subsequent to verbal pressure, threats to end the relationship, or false promises," among others, all equivalent to sexual assault. Of course, raptorial feints like threats and false promises can work both ways, but Koss cannot admit any form of parity.

Koss then offers the bedazzled reader a tsunami of different categories of rape, to wit: individual rape, pair rape, multiple rape, stranger rape, acquaintance rape, date rape, marital rape, partially planned rape, unplanned rape, reported rape, campus rape, hidden rape and so on—though she neglects to mention the trauma from which she herself evidently suffers, namely, rape on the brain. And of course, in today's feminist climate, an inebriated woman who has sex is counted as a rape victim; her inebriated male partner is regarded—and prosecuted—as the perpetrator, as the notorious Brock Turner rape case at Stanford made clear. The man always takes advantage of the woman. The woman never takes advantage of the man. According to the feminists, female compliance is almost always a consequence of male coercion.

What is now obvious is that the standard exaggerations simply do not hold. The American College Health Association in its 2017 survey of campus life reported non-consensual sexual penetration among female students at 3%. "Penetration" may not necessarily mean what it implies; intimate touching, caressing or probing is also defined as "penetration." Of course, this is a survey whose categories are already extremely vague; for example, non-consent is often a retroactive consideration. Days or weeks after a sexual encounter, a woman may feel she had been pressured or "guilted" and therefore did not really consent. She then files a complaint which is accepted literally by campus authorities since her actual compliance or state of self-induced intoxication is not regarded as a contributing element. After all, yes doesn't always mean yes.

In its Executive Summary for Spring 2016, the *National College Health Assessment* for the province of Ontario, where my wife teaches at a major university, assigns a value of 2.6% for its "sexual penetration without their consent" category. At the same time the Academic Impacts section states that only 1.3% of students considered "Assault (sexual)" as affecting their academic performance. In either case, the ratio is not even close to the 33% figure cited by political bloviators like Andrea Horwath.

It gets worse—or better, depending on your viewpoint. The Special Report for 1995-2013 issued by the U.S. Department of Justice actually reduces the rape tally to .6%, that is, from 330 per 1000 as the feminists and social justice types claim to 6.1 per 1000. Still too much, of course, but better less than 1% than over 30%. The problem, too, as we have seen, is that the concept of rape has been stretched so thin as to include even the most normal initiative or innocuous gesture. In this case, the real statistics for college rape victims should probably be pegged at one out of one, or 100%.

One of the most important and enduring books on the subject is Christina Hoff Sommers' *Who Stole Feminism?*, published in 1994, in which she analyzes Koss's unsound approach and advocacy research in the latter's study of sexual assault. Since Koss holds that rape, as she wrote in her 1985 *Ms Magazine* article "The Hidden Rape Victim," "is on a continuum with normal male behavior," even fondling or petting may constitute sexual victimization. Further, fully 73% of Koss's ostensible rape victims did not believe they had been raped, but Koss's method "allows the surveyor to decide whether a rape occurred," a very handy *modus operandi*. The problem is that Koss and her congeners, as Sommers demonstrates, design their questionnaires to yield high numbers. Low figures generate no headlines.

The reputable studies Sommers consults that disarmed the stratospheric numbers of sexually victimized campus females appeared in the early 80s, yet in 2018 the inflated calculus is graven in many university brochures and pamphlets. The *USA Today* article cited above features an image of Stanford students wearing mortarboards marked 1/3. How explain this anomaly?

For one thing, radical feminists will without compunction use outright lies, dodgy statistics and obscurantist dogma to advance their inflammatory message that American (and Canadian) culture is sexist, misogynist and patriarchal, and that the university is a seething pit of male predation. And students and staff have bitten into the nothing burger. For another, the rape crisis movement is largely a function of privilege. College girls, stemming primarily from middle and upper middle class families, are a comparatively pampered group who are accustomed to or expect favored treatment, even if the threat is practically non-existent; their counterparts in poor areas and blue collar districts, Sommers points out, receive little attention or funding.

Campus rape is an ideological fairy tale, the negative image of genuine fairy tales which, as Faith Moore writes in *PJ Media*, "have their own symbolic code…to reveal a universal truth," namely, "the good is beautiful." The feminist fairy tale teaches the opposite: fear, aggression and hatred—in effect, the beautiful is bad. The handsome prince is a rapist at heart rather than a symbol of beneficial transformation.

I think it is fair to say, following a judicious review of the methodologies in play, the misandrist agenda of the militant feminists and the empirical evidence of the senses, that the feminist data are utterly fraudulent. After listening to the ideologues, the trolls, the man-haters, the snowflakes, the journalists, the counselors, the "experts," the politicians, the spineless college administrators and the rest of what novelist Thomas Pynchon called "the whole sick crew," one might be inclined to avail oneself of the new analgesic now on the market for beleaguered parents, but which surely allows for multiple purposes and applications. Just ask the pharmacist for a bottle of AphukenbrakE. It's a start.

The Map of Love and Misreading

The Anglo-Egyptian novelist Ahdaf Soueif is not a bad writer but she's not a very good one either. Her reputation rests mainly on one book, *The Map of Love*, which sold over a million copies and was shortlisted for the 1999 Man Booker Prize, and featured on some tendentious and partisan political journalism for *The Guardian*. What unites her fiction and her journalism is an overt sympathy for the Palestinians—she was the founder of the annual Palestine Festival of Literature—and a corresponding hostility toward Israel. Clearly, these are political attitudes that endear her to a literary establishment and wide readership who share these conventional leftwing and pro-Islamic sentiments, and which may partially account for the book's success.

Publishers Weekly anoints Soueif as "the intellectual heir of Edward Said," and there is certainly a slight modicum of truth to this promotion to the ranks of influence and repute. In her slanted and one-sided *Guardian* essay, "Under the Gun," collected in Mezzaterra: Fragments from the Common Ground, she laments that her life "has been overcast by the shadow of Israel," proceeds to reduce the complex nature of Israeli-Palestinian relations to the dimensions of a fairy tale, misrepresents UN Resolution 242 in passing, and raises the 2000 Intifada to the heights of an epic struggle of the pristinely innocent against the barbarously guilty. For Soueif, "the discord between the Arab world and the U.S. is entirely to do with Israel," aping the palpably flawed position associated with Said and his followers like John Mearsheimer and Stephen Walt in their shabbily confected *The Israel Lobby*. Soueif does her best to advance and popularize such gross distortions of truth in both her commentary and her fiction.

Notes from a Derelict Culture

The Map of Love pushes all the right buttons in the great console of ready-made opinion that prevails today. It purports to be a love story unfolding on several parallel historical planes, set a century apart in colonial and modern Egypt. An English widow, Anne Winterbourne, moves to Egypt and falls in love with an irredentist radical, Sharif Pasha al-Baroudi, whom she marries in 1901. In 1997, her great granddaughter, Isabel Parkman, embarks from New York on a journey to Egypt to trace her family history, and falls in love with the symphony conductor and activist Omar al-Ghamrawi who has embraced the Palestinian cause, an obvious surrogate for Edward Said. The novel is admittedly rich in evocative description but is fatally weakened by an air of romantic sensationalism, an *haut goût* of maudlin evangelism and an insinuating current of predictable disinformation.

Soueif's novel brings to mind another cartographical production, Harold Bloom's celebrated critical volume, *A Map of Misreading* (a companion to *The Anxiety of Influence*). Among the various litcrit categories or "revisionary ratios" that Bloom develops we find one he names "Apophrades" (from the Greek for "impure days," inauspicious events"), which he redefines as a form of poetic and literary influence resembling "the Return of the Dead"—the great writers of the past who haunt and intimidate the present-day author with precisely their greatness. What Bloom calls "the imagination's struggle with its own origins" leads to the imagination surrendering to a "teleological error," its projected ends marred by a faulty and melodramatic reading of both its past and its present.

In the case of *The Map of Love*, the structure of the device is repeated on the plane of narrative. The writer constructs a false tableau of the *now* that is meant to subsume and transcend the sentimental ideal of the *then*. It is, in effect, an impure or inauspicious transaction. A supposedly exalted past when men were heroic and larger than life and women were wise and adventurous is reprised and strengthened in a simulating present.

Within the tissue of the narrative, Omar is clearly a contemporary update of the exotic, fearless, and tribally dedicated Sharif, as if Soueif were enacting a parody of the primal scene of Freudian repetition, or in Bloom's terminology, as if she had invested in "the compulsion to repeat the precursor's patterns" in an attempt "to recover the prestige of origins…since such mediation holds open the perpetual possibility of one's own sublimity." Omar's sublimity, however, is not persuasive; it is simply posited by authorial fiat. Indeed, Soueif's stock in trade seems to be a manufactured glamour painted onto wooden characters.

But beyond the boundaries of the novel, as we have noted, Omar is intended to suggest Edward Said. He represents Soueif's deceptive and largely untenable effort to valorize a literary and cultural giant who is now coming increasingly to look like the petty, hypocritical and mendacious doyen of a generation of leftwing postmodern intellectuals. *The Map of Love* is, finally, little more than a pulpy yet insidious piece of Islamic and Palestinian special pleading and a sorry attempt to rescue the endangered reputation of a morally tainted and intellectually dishonest scholar.

I wish to avoid Bloomian technicalities. Simply put, apophrades is the mode of thought which brings a dominant, commanding and *idealized* past into the given moment in order to create an even greater and more ennobled present. This imaginary time-transfer, Bloom warns, creates a present which subsequently vanishes between the two antithetical poles of the "past-in-the-future" (e.g., a projected restored Caliphate) and "the future-in-the-past" (e.g., a wished-for 7th century revival), which is exactly the historical dilemma of contemporary Islam and, *mutatis mutandis*, of the Palestinian dream world. The Palestinian *nomenklatura* presupposes an ancient people and an idealized nation that never existed but which is taken as a past reality. This bogus construct is then elevated into a conceptual present which promises to be a restoration, a fulfillment and, ultimately, an even grander and more resilient political fact. But the possible and *sustainable* present — a viable, democratic and prosperous sovereign state living in peace with its neighbor — is lost in the gap between an apocryphal memory and a spurious future.

In *The Map of Love*, Ahdaf Soueif is playing the apophradic game, conjuring the Return of the Dead — or the Return of the Illusory — to affront the living with impossibility. On one level a literary artifact, it is on another, deeper level a subliminal political manifesto. She establishes an equation or "revisionary ratio" between 19th century England and Egypt on the one hand and modern Israel and "Palestine" on the other, all the while touting Edward Said as the visionary leader and prophet who labors for a desired future. As Egypt eventually triumphed in its quest for independence at the expense of imperial Britain, so "Palestine" will presumably realize its successful struggle against Israeli oppression, as Said urged and assumed in *The Question of Palestine* and other books.

That the equation is invalid, that the Palestinians never constituted a coherent and hereditary people, that their past and their future have no common boundary in a feasible or workable present, and that Israel, according to international law, the laws of war and facts on the ground, is not an occupying power—all this has no purchase on what is essentially, to cite Bloom again, a phony substitution of "early for late and late for early."

Meanwhile, Soueif has done her tawdry and clandestine job, to nobody's advantage except perhaps her own and those who gain from pushing the Palestinian fable. The map of love is really a map of misreading. A false prophet is given messianic credibility and a rich and productive present falls between the antipodes of a corrupted past and an anterior future.

Gnostics of Our Time

A perhaps surprising relation exists between a branch of ancient Christian theology (or anti-theology) and a modern secular political movement, that is, between Gnosticism and Left-Liberal progressivism. In tracing this oddly creedal linkage, it will be helpful to begin with a brief and broad-stroke analysis of the Gnostic doctrine before appraising its application to the political sensibility of the Left. These two phenomena share a similar psychological matrix and both are fueled by the paradoxical theory of what we might call "pastoral insurgency."

The term *Gnosticism* refers technically to various heretical sects of the first six Christian centuries that taught that knowledge (Greek: *gnosis*) rather than faith was the key to salvation. But such knowledge was, in effect, a putative and esoteric insight into the nature of the Creation which understood the existence of evil not as a product of man's free will but as a flaw inherent in the very origin of the cosmos. Mankind has got things backwards. The fault lies with the Creator. The snake is our misprized benefactor who comes with knowledge of salvation, wisdom and healing, as we now find its remedial emblem on the medical caduceus. Which is to say that mankind has been the victim of a diabolical stratagem, seduced by a devious "cosmocrator" into seeing what is evil as good and what is good as evil.

As I understand it, the essence of Gnosticism is this: *the natural is regarded as unnatural.* The laws of nature—aging, suffering, death, competition between individuals, groups and species for resources and living space—are perceived as the consequence of a Divine mistake or a Demonic usurpation. Something went wrong at the moment of Creation, violating the immanent design latent in the "singularity."

The world is not as initially intended and is therefore repudiated as unnatural, an aberration.

According to Kurt Rudolph, one of the leading specialists of the subject and author of *Gnosis: The Nature and History of Gnosticism*, we are treating of a "dualistic religion…which took up a definitely negative attitude towards the world and the society of the time, and proclaimed a deliverance of man precisely from the constraints of earthly existence into his essential relationship…with a supramundane realm of freedom." This pre-flaw, supramundane realm could only be entered via an existential rejection of remarkable proportions, which Rudolph describes in his conclusion as "too hostile to the world."

The remedies proposed to combat and counteract the flaw in the Creation were multifarious and not always in agreement with one another—there are several different flavors of Gnosticism. But the common denominator was the conviction, to quote from David Horowitz's acute essay on the subject, that "redemption does not lie in the fulfillment of the moral covenants and adherence to the law, but in the abolition and 'transcendence' of both." The world and all its customs, beliefs, norms, usages and statutes was disavowed as a vast and perverse deception. The imperative was to restore a prior or potential, but shattered, harmony by whatever means necessary and thus to *recreate the Creation*.

The Gnostic vision was later taken up by the more familiar Lurianic Kabbalah with its injunction to repair the world—*tikkun olam*—so that the "shattering of the vessels" of Creation could be undone and the fragments retrieved from the abyss into which they had fallen, and finally annealed. But Kabbalah is a non-aggressive philosophy and may be characterized as Gnosticism-lite, as it were. For Kabbalah, the world can be redeemed through faith and right conduct, metaphorized as the gleaning of the broken shards of the universal frame; for Gnosticism, the world as we know it cannot be saved but must be reconstituted. It must be demolished and re-made from the ground up. It must, as Philip Gardiner writes in *Gnosis*, restore the embodied temple of "the perfected man."

Gnostics of Our Time

Enter the Left, which didn't just spring up in the writings of Rousseau or Marx or in the French National Assembly of 1789, where members of the revolutionary Third Estate sat on the left side of the chamber. Its mindset has been with us at least since the advent of Gnosticism, a major locus of subsequent dissemination. Its influence on the history of thought is widespread and announces itself in different dimensions. Horowitz writes: "Just as religious gnosticism sees evil as a flaw in the cosmic creation, so secular gnosticism sees evil as a flaw in the social cosmos." "In this revolutionary mysticism," he continues, "the messianic liberator is imprisoned in capitalist darkness…This mysticism is at the heart of every movement that seeks a revolutionary transformation of the world we know." For the most part, today's Western intellectuals and academics, governing elites, NGOs and, generally speaking, our Left-oriented, official culture are the heirs of the Gnostic theologians of the early Christian era.

The ideology of the Left, then, may be described as an *adaptive* political expression of the Gnostic sensibility, a kind of retro revival. There are residual differences, of course. But all of the Left's diverse manifestations, from radical communism to the more complaisant forms of soft-focus socialism, are actuated by the mystical lure of a harmonious society posited as the end-goal of History—a society in which the elements of conflict have been banished and sufficient wherewithal is assured for all its members. The Hegelian assumption—partially adopted by Marx—of the "end" toward which the forces of History are tending is the secular version of the Gnostic reverie of the benign blueprint that was somehow botched. (For Hegel, as might be expected, the dialectical journey toward perfection comes to fulfillment in Berlin.) The Leftist dream of ultimate "ends" mirrors the Gnostic illusion of first beginnings, of a pre-existent purpose. For this psychology, only the Ideal is Real, and the Real is recognized as something that is opposed to the actual, to what is presently the case.

Whether we are considering the Gnostic kernel-thought of cosmic revisionism; or the Marxist-Socialist doctrine of social rehabilitation; or the current global warming hysteria which aims for the restoration of a pre-industrial planet; or the mental sedatives known as the doctrines of "social justice" and "universal human rights" which, as Daniel Hannan elaborates in *The New Road to Serfdom*, have nothing to do with new rights but with institutional centralization and international organizations that "get to determine what our rights are"; or the Obamantra of "hope and change" and all that it implies of redistributive economics, what we are observing is the perpetual march of human folly. It will stop at nothing—neither dogmatic ignorance, nor cultivated nihilism, nor imaginary resolutions, nor planned upheaval, nor destructive violence—to construct a pristine simulacrum of the Gnostic hallucination as if it were a viable alternative to the world as it fundamentally is and always will be. To apply the words of Paul Auster in *Moon Palace*, "This was imagination in its purest form, the act…of persuading others to accept a world that was not really there."

Absurd and ruinous as it may be, the Gnostic prepossession—to give it its due—absolves human beings of responsibility for primal evil, realizing the contradiction embedded in traditional theodicy: a God with absolute foreknowledge of the results of unpredictable human free will. To their credit, the Gnostics recognized that determinism and freedom cannot be reconciled—a "revelation" that appears to have escaped not only the general run of classical theologians but the purveyors of the historical dialectic for whom the goal of history is pre-scripted. This is one of the distinctions between the Gnostics and their seminal Leftist successors. The similarities, however, outweigh the differences.

At this juncture, it must be fairly admitted that there is a sense in which we are all garden-variety Gnostics, concerned with good design in the objects and services we rely on. As Donald Norman acknowledges in *The Psychology of Everyday Things*, "Proper design can make a difference in the quality of life," and when the design of the things we use proves defective, we should "write to manufacturers" and "boycott unusable designs." The Gnostics, of course, were preoccupied with everyday life, but on a far grander scale than the average consumer. Their theological treatises and discourses might be construed as forms of writing to the Manufacturer and their pronouncements and activities as a way of boycotting an unusable or, at least, an unacceptable design implicit in the cosmos itself. It was not a teapot or window latch or door handle they wished to redesign, but the entire created universe. By thus exceeding their mandate (to use a current phrase), they inevitably succumbed to the self-defeating pitfall of hubris.

Nevertheless, before dismissing Gnosticism out of hand and in an effort to understand it better in order to track the danger it represents, we need to see that it is rooted in the perennial human desire for a better world, a nature no longer red in tooth and claw, a society of men in which all the necessities of life are provided equally to all, and an international arena in which nations regard themselves as peaceable members of the larger human family. This is the point of contact between Gnosticism and the Left. It is a noble fantasy in the abstract, but disastrous in its implementation. For the world doesn't, never has, and never will work this way. Inequality is inevitable (even in a "classless" society), competition is incessant (even in a "worker's paradise"), and violence is unavoidable (within or between nations). These are the "laws" of human nature that cannot be evaded. The only reasonable response to an interminably flawed human Creation is cautious and pragmatic, that is, the attempt to *reduce* ineliminable suffering by gradual, empirical methods. The road to a better future is both asymptotic and rutted, but it is preferable to a razed landscape.

The Gnostic epigones of the Left do not see it this way. In his recent *Ameritopia*, Mark Levin quotes Friedrich Hayek's *The Road to Serfdom* that the aim of such political utopians "is no less than to effect a complete redesigning of our traditional morals, law, and language, and on this basis to stamp out the older order and supposedly inexorable, unjustifiable conditions that prevent the institution of reason, fulfillment, true freedom, and justice." Political utopianism, Levin comments, "is tyranny disguised as a desirable, workable, and even paradisiacal ideology." Political utopianism is the way in which the Gnostic compulsion has been domesticated in the modern age.

For, rather than deal with the world in all its complexities and resistances, the Gnostic premise of a pre-existent plenitude that must be recovered morphs into the utopian conviction of an ideal civil and political substitute for things as they are. The means to achieve this vision, as millions have learned to their cost, is a species of top-down collectivism administered by a cabal of "experts," theorists, intellectuals, technocrats and political strongmen for whom tradition, tested precedent and moral standards are anathema. As author of *Shakedown Socialism* Oleg Atbashian points out, a corollary of this arrangement is that the blame for its inevitable miscarriage can be, like a society's wealth, illicitly redistributed. "Collectivism provides us with a sufficiently analgesic illusion of fairness." Responsibility for failure will fall on "those close to you, or on an unfair system, or even on the big wide (and deeply flawed) world."

There can be little doubt that the suffering caused by the Gnostic disease is immeasurable, for the world is not amenable to radical transformation. Nature remains predatory and omnivorous—"this munching universe," as Lawrence Durrell put it in his Gnostic fiction *Monsieur, or The Prince of Darkness*. Human society is capable of slow ameliorative change through scientific advancements and wise political legislation respectful of human rights and freedoms, but it will never escape the orbit of imparity and dissension in which it moves. Nonetheless, the rational enterprise of gradual and empirical renovation within natural limits is not attractive to the neo-Leftist romantic idealist, mired as he is in a state of unmitigated hubris. His energy goes into the projection of a civil Shangri-La without contour and substance to be constructed upon the debris of the very liberal democracy and free market economy which have provided him with life, livelihood and, in many instances, professional honour.

As Eric Voegelin writes in *The New Science of Politics*, a profound analysis of the ideological misconceptions that vitiate the political thought and practice of the contemporary West, the utopian answer to the Gnostic concept of an original evil is the chief hazard of our professional political and academic classes. These classes are plainly susceptible to the virus of "theoretical illiteracy," which shows itself in "the form of various social idealisms" or an "axiological dream world." In short, the Gnostic enthusiast wishes to replace the civil order with a uncivil theology. For this oddly hermetic temperament, says Voegelin, the "nonrecognition of reality is the first principle." This is the best definition of the political Left one can hope to find.

To conclude. The psychology of the Left, despite certain asymmetries, is intrinsically a Gnostic one. The analogy is premonitory. For just as Gnosticism proved unsustainable as a resilient and effective theology, since it could not address the needs of the human spirit bound in time to an ineluctable world, so the theory of utopian socialism that animates the orphic community, in any of its manifold incarnations, can only distort the quest for human betterment. It can only reproduce — or worsen — the original flaw it seeks to transcend.

An Interview with ....

Our guest today is Dr. Manfred Aufgeblasener-Schwätzer, director of the Nationales Klima Zentrum (National Climate Center) in Hamburg, Germany. A world-famous climatologist, he is a staunch believer in anthropogenic global warming and has worked closely with the Hadley Climate Research Unit and the Goddard Institute for Space Studies.

DS: Manfred Aufgeblasener-Schwätzer, Thank you for agreeing to this interview.

M.A-S: I am honored.

DS: You are aware, of course, of the scandal unfolding at the Hadley CRU and elsewhere, popularly referred to as Climategate. What do you make of this?

M.A-S: It is all nonsense, obviously, a minor—how do you say it in English?—a minor blip. The science is settled. The world is warming even as we speak, moment by moment. Averaged over a decade, the result is alarming. Over a century, it is catastrophic. The prospect of planetary heat-death makes one shudder and gives one nightmares. I have developed a great sensitivity over the years of my work at the Zentrum to the slightest variations in temperature. I see it not only in my computer models and mathematical graphs but can actually feel it on the back of my neck and at times over my entire body, as if I am trapped in a Swedish sauna.

DS: But surely the leaked emails and files indicating collusion among the various scientists involved, the suppression or distortion of critical data, the pressure levied against scientific journals to exclude the work of "climate skeptics," the preselection of weather stations to inflate temperature records, the misuse of tree ring data, the sloppy note-taking, the loss or deletion of vast amounts of archival material, the absorption of unrefereed articles, and so on, must signify that a massive scam has been perpetrated on an unsuspecting public.

M.A-S: Not at all. Not at all. You cannot believe what you read in the blogosphere. It is all lies, I tell you, lies. And people are so naive and sometimes even disrespectful of the world's great scientists. Was not Galileo threatened for his discoveries and forced to recant? Is not my friend, the esteemed Dr. Phil Jones at the Hadley, being cruelly attacked even as we speak for his major insights and crucial breakthroughs? The world is growing hotter by the moment and if we do not act very soon, then before we know it there shall be no more icebergs, the islands of the Pacific will sink like rusty submarines, Greenland will become a desert, lobsters will cook in the oceans, volcanoes will boil over, the Arctic will become a spa, Holland will vanish—it is too horrible to contemplate. I have seen reports this very morning that the permafrost is dissolving and the frozen peat bogs are turning to sponge beneath the feet of Canada's Inuit and Finland's Laplander populations. My collaborator Dr. James Hansen of NASA foretells that New York City will be under fifty feet of water in just two or three generations, and he is an acclaimed expert. We would be foolish to challenge his word.

DS: But Dr. Aufgeblasener-Schwätzer, we now have reputable and undoubted evidence that there has been no global warming for more than a decade, and indeed the mean average temperature has actually declined by .07 degrees.

M.A-S.: Lies, I tell you. You cannot trust contradictory evidence.

Whatever goes against the current consensus is plainly a mischievous effort to undermine the credibility of our selfless scientists. In truth, what we are seeing is a conspiracy generated by anti-scientific frauds who refuse to accept what we are telling them and who will do anything to discredit genuine scientific analysis and malign the integrity of our dedicated researchers.

DS: But what would these so-called skeptics have to gain by their resistance?

M.A-S: That is another issue. I do not have the facts, but I suspect it is world domination and the exploitation of the poor, the secret agenda of western capitalism whose sinister purpose these frauds and skeptics willingly serve.

DS: Well, be that as it may, what is your informed opinion regarding the Medieval Warming Period? New studies appear to suggest it was warmer then, or at least as warm as it is today, which would seriously compromise official assessments that we are living in unprecedented times.

M.A-S: That is complete nonsense. After all, we were not there, so how can we really know? We have no sworn affidavits from the period, therefore speculation is, as we say, unwarranted. But I must be fair. There is indeed one document dating from the time, attributed to Frater Wolfgang the Amanuensis from the Cistercian Monastery at Maulbronn, who claimed that the days were "as hot as hell" and that the Fiend would shortly make his *parousia*, his demonic advent. But this is clearly the fantasy of a crazy scriptorium dweller.

DS: Let's change the subject. You were an important participant at the Copenhagen Climate Conference. Many are now saying it ended in failure. Would you agree?

M.A-S: Not at all.

DS: Why would that be?

M.A-S: Copenhagen was a step in the right direction, as was Kyoto. We will now accelerate the process. Copenhagen was an opportunity for the world's best thinkers, such as the respected Al Gore, and the world's most enlightened statesmen, such as Barack Obama, Robert Mugabe and Hugo Chavez, to get to know one another, to find themselves, as you say in English, on the same page, and to work together for the greater good of mankind. We must be grateful for their heroic efforts.

DS: Then you consider Copenhagen a success?

M.A-S: Oh yes, definitely. If you will permit me a moment of levity. You know, one of my favorite American movies is *Hans Christian Andersen* with your famous Danny Kaye. I often hum to myself his marvelous song "Wonderful Copenhagen." Just as in the song, we were all clinking glasses " 'neath her tavern light," for Copenhagen, as he sang, is really a "friendly old girl of a town." And indeed we made many friends there, 45,000 to be exact. So there is no doubt we will succeed. We have the numbers.

DS: You certainly do have the numbers. Though many say the numbers were woven out of whole cloth.

M.A-S: Please?

DS: My moment of levity. I mean, that the numbers coming out of Hadley and Goddard were concocted, invented, made up.

M.A-S: Do not believe that for an instant. Is not the United Nations solidly behind our results? Has not Dr. Rajendra Pachauri, chairman of the IPCC and my most trusted colleague, supported us with his immense authority and knowledge? Yes, yes, I am aware that he said the Himalayan glaciers would melt practically overnight. But you must understand that Dr. Pachauri, driven by the urgency of the situation, was merely trying to provoke quick, concerted action. It was a noble attempt which has been much misunderstood. I know, too, that he has been unfairly censured for his connections to various commercial enterprises involved in transactions dealing with climate affairs. But these relations are entirely disinterested and are intended to prepare the human race for sustainable existence.

DS: What do you make of Dr. Michael Mann's celebrated "hockey stick" graph showing a precipitous spike in current temperatures? Has it not been exposed as a consequence of data-tampering and thoroughly exploded?

M.A-S: No, no, no. That is a vile smear circulated by those who do not understand the complexities of minute calibrations, draught simulations, projected adjustments and the proper manipulation of hockey sticks. They insist on holding the hockey stick *down*, as it were, so that the blade is parallel with the ice surface. Whereas Dr. Mann in conformity with his findings holds the *shaft* of the hockey stick parallel to the ice surface, allowing the blade to rise skyward. You realize, of course, that climate hockey is not the same as ice hockey.

DS: What is your perspective on programs such as carbon offsets, cap and trade, wealth transfers to underprivileged countries, and the like? Do you believe they will have an adverse effect on the economies of First World nations, as critics have warned?

M.A-S: An excellent question. Let me reply with a question. Do not Third World nations deserve to be subsidized by the rapacious and polluting nations of the west, even if these latter should become Third World nations themselves? This would be only economic justice, a goal toward which we must all work with one mind, regardless of the sacrifice to our lifestyle. We must learn to live with deprivation. And as we know, these programs are utterly necessary to contribute to the reduction of CO_2 that is choking our future and to bring about the greening of the environment. Can you not envision a world in which smokestacks and furnaces and automobiles will be replaced by windmills and solar panels and rickshaws, a world of punitive energy costs whose industrial engine will inevitably slow down and perhaps stop altogether? Utopia on earth!

DS: So, to conclude, you have no doubt that the planet is warming and that the significant factor, as the climate community has claimed, is man-caused atmospheric CO_2.

M.A-S: Absolutely. You must read my paper in the Russian journal *RIA Novosti*, "Vertical Symmetry Structures and Decadal Sinusoidal Fluctuations as Amplification Vectors: Establishing Greenhouse Correlations Over Temporal Motility Scales." It will convince you. And I refer you once again to Herr Gore who bravely testified before your Senate Foreign Relations Committee in January 2009 that the Earth is racing toward Venus-type CO_2 levels. True, the atmosphere of Venus is composed of 97% CO_2 while that of the Earth is .038%. But do not be deceived. Owing to what we call "CO_2 forcing," a chemical chain reaction producing a multiplier effect, the differential will close rapidly. Our descendants will fry like wienerschnitzel. It is not, as you Americans say, a pretty picture.

DS: Manfred Aufgeblasener-Schwätzer, thank you again for being our guest today. Would you have anything to add before we close this interview?

M.A-S: Yes. It is very hot in here.

The Wild Hunt

One of the popular strains of our protracted adolescent sub-culture is called live-action-role playing, or LARP, a type of gaming based on the obsessive need to escape the rigors and constraints of the real world. It involves the fantasy substitutions of roles and personae for the humdrum identities of our own recalcitrant natures. Online avatars are a more passive instance of this desire to transcend the limitations of the self and the captive circumstances of everyday life. But live-action-role-playing brings the passion for this evasion of and deliverance from the quotidian to a whole new level of engagement.

A recent movie dramatizes the LARP phenomenon to perfection. *The Wild Hunt* is a shoestring-budget Canadian production based on an ancient Norse myth recounting the exploits of a group of phantasmal warriors thundering across the skies. Somewhat more modestly, the film tells the story of a band of young men and women playing at being a troupe of Vikings and Celts and other mytho-historical characters somewhere in the northern forests of Quebec. They adopt heroic names, loll about on fur couches, wear magical cloaks, quaff beakers of ale, dance around bonfires, speak in archaic idioms, invoke the gods, and sally forth to storm castles and wage harmless combat with one another. When chided for the absurdity of his caperings, one of the participants replies, "Well, at least we're fun losers." He could not have been more wrong.

Eventually, as real-life relationships begin to emerge in all their untameable complexity, the innocence of the game is lost, jealousies and antagonisms break through the surface of theatrical posturing, and one of the players is gruesomely murdered, his head smashed repeatedly against a rock. Fantasy can never keep reality at bay for very long, which inevitably intrudes with a vengeance. The director's message is clear. Live-action-role-playing—in effect, a vivid kind of pretending—is a temporary reprieve from the grimly ineluctable world that we find so hard to accept but must come to terms with to ward off unanticipated disaster.

In order to avoid abstraction, we should try to specify what we mean by "reality." To say *without qualification* that reality is simply "what is" plainly won't do, since pretending also *is* and functions as an element of the given. What we mean in the deeper sense by "what is" requires some amplification. Reality, I would suggest, is defined for us by *the advent of the irreversible*. Ageing and death are inescapable, unless one is Dorian Gray or Elijah. We cannot go back in time unless we live in an H.G. Wells story or a Michael J. Fox movie. We cannot undo what has been done. We cannot become someone else no matter how hard we may try. In the fantasy world, such things may be possible, but in the real world, regrettably, one cannot underclock and do things over again to create a preferred outcome.

That is precisely why a miracle is a miracle: it purports to reverse in the real world what can only be reversed in fiction, dream or mythology. Lazarus can return from the dead and Orpheus from the underworld. The sun can stand still "in the midst of the heavens" to ensure a military victory. Destiny can be thwarted, if you inhabit Spanish playwright Pedro Calderón's *Life Is a Dream*. Groundhog Day can recycle indefinitely to enable the revision of stubborn events. Infinitely recurring simulations, or Source Codes, can adjust the structure of impending reality. One can step into an obverse, looking-glass world where everything is done differently. Miracles—at whatever level of importance they are thought to occur—are subsidized by the powerful human desire to commute reality in favor of the counterfactual and thus to transform or reverse the settled order of the mundane.

Of course, change is a part of life and nature, but there is no eluding the fact that change is also a refractory part of existence and cannot be reversed. Change is an unchangeable aspect of the real and is always unidirectional. In the real world retroversion is contra-indicated—which is what we intuitively understand by "reality." The constitutive "nature of things" cannot be remade. Though we all know this, the trouble is that we often act as if we didn't and continually invest in one or another form of live-action-role-playing. No harm done if the illusion is kept under strict control and readily exited; otherwise the losing will not be fun.

The dilemma is obviously compounded when live-action-role-playing becomes a staple of political life and infects the foreign policy of entire national administrations. Enacting a LARP-like geopolitical fantasy on the international stage must invariably produce destructive consequences. Neville Chamberlain, who played the role of the peace maker and assumed that Hitler was a fellow actor, learned that sanguinary lesson to his and his nation's exorbitant cost, as did the rest of the world—some fifty to seventy million dead. The results of Chamberlain's folly were irreversible, no less so than is the presence of evil in the world, as he should have expected had he possessed the merest ounce of realism and been able to grasp the "vectors" of human nature. The "anatomy of appeasement," writes Bruce Thornton in his *The Wages of Appeasement*, discounts "the permanent truths of human nature expressed through social and political mechanisms."

Indulging in the premise that Islam is a religion of peace, for example, and not a determined theo-political enemy is an untenable fantasy. Yet far too many still play the game of interfaith dialogue and sympathetic outreach, some changing their names and embracing the five pillars, others supporting building mosques even on inappropriate ground, still others believing that an "Arab Spring" is not what it ominously portended, that is, a fundamentalist winter.

Similarly, to plunge one's country into insurmountable debt in the conviction that everything will work out at the end of the day is to swing in a basket in Cloud-Cuckoo Land. To say, as did Canadian Prime Minister Justin Trudeau that "the economy will balance itself" is pure LARP. To print fiat money and suppose that the currency will not be debased is to court the miraculous. Pretending that the United Nations is a fount of hope for a better world and not the cauldron of iniquity that it actually is can lead only to grief and destitution. To believe that relations with an autocratic adversary can be summarily "reset" in defiance of his obvious interests and purposes is to run about donning horned helmets and waving wooden swords in the northern forests of Quebec. To argue that the climate is warming when it is actually cooling, thanks to a Solar Minimum, is to play ostrich with a vengeance.

The way things are cannot be modded, as if we were dealing with a piece of software, a computer game, a steampunk novel or a provisory masquerade intended to generate an altered content. In short, to behave as if something is not what it *irreversibly is in real time and real life* is a sure-fire way of offending the iron-willed gods who rule the world and bringing down nemesis upon our heads.

This is why the West, snagged in its own shambolic variant of the wild hunt, is in serious trouble and may not survive the depredations of the real world which it can neither understand nor counter. Open borders, illegal immigration, massive importation of third-world refugees, global governance, single-payer medicare, abortion at will, endlessly renewable energy via sun and wind, redistributive economics, "social justice" levelling, climate warming, programmatic feminism — all aspects of a vast imaginary production, acting as if the world is not what it intractably is and staging what can only be described as a risible and emptily flamboyant performance, though one which casts a dark and lengthening shadow. We dash about brandishing our fantasies and delusions, unaware that the world is not kind to its fugitives and deniers. For such people, to quote Rush Limbaugh, "Failure is a résumé enhancement."

The truth is, the Western world is involved in live-action role-playing, that is, in mounting a destructive fiction. But it is only a matter of time before reality announces its implacable presence and the LARP game collapses in ruins around us. For the LARPist cannot reverse the remorseless trajectory of history or re-invent the way the world works.

We are busily acting in *The Wild Hunt II*. And the sequel will be catastrophic.

On Making Love and Having Sex

In our time the task of understanding ourselves is perpetually frustrated by the almost instinctive blending we make of two contradictory modes of being: the mechanical and the spiritual. Because we are short on spiritual reality we are long on mechanical models. We confuse the instantaneity of the computer with the timelessness of genuine insight. We think of memory as a form of storage, learning as efficient programming, education as the acquisition of skills and techniques, harmony as smooth functioning, self-development as the accumulation of isolable and multiple capacities like a Black & Decker kitchen-center or a Swiss Army knife, self-expression as a kind of accelerator-pushing to burn off excess fumes. And—the cardinal sin—we consider spirit itself as the free exercise of charity in exactly the same way as a mechanism must be used from time to time without a designated purpose in order not to jam with rust or dust. Our attitude to the supersensible is basically hygienic.

When the Duke in Browning's "My Last Duchess" says that he refuses to stoop to indicate to his wife just what adjustments to make in her conduct in order to settle his doubts and so preserve the marriage, he is articulating a fundamental humanism. Today we merely visit a counselor, a.k.a. a gender reconciliation facilitator, who listens, ruminates, tinkers, and offers recommendations to repair a marriage gone on the blink—much as a garage mechanic puts his ear to the hood, plays with the engine, quotes various alternatives, and concludes by replacing a few parts to get the buggy on the road again. What we have done is assimilate the evangelical mystery of marriage to the intricate functioning of a twelve-tappet, fuel-injected turbo-Jag. Snafty and impressive as this may be, it is still just a metal case with a lot of repetitively moving parts.

Even the psyche is compared to elaborate mechanical or objective paradigms. For Karl Jung the soul is a telluric mound which must be excavated by the psycho-archeologist who wishes to penetrate to ever deeper levels. For Freud it is a huge and complicated hydraulic system with its pressure-chambers, reservoirs and manifold displacements. To paraphrase French philosopher Gabriel Marcel, it is not a mystery, merely a problem. Psychic health is simply a matter of getting the defective item into the diagnostic clinic and making the appropriate adjustments—unless, of course, the whole engine has seized and fused upon itself in an irreversible psychotic meld.

I am not speaking here of the inveterate and beneficial tendency of language to diffract its meanings through the prism of metaphor. Metaphor, as everyone knows, is the semantic substratum of language and all real communication is paradigmatic in nature. We think and utter in terms of models, figures and comparisons, effortlessly and unconsciously. What I am drawing attention to is the prodigious emphasis we have placed on one particular category of experience whenever we think about ourselves or our relationships. I don't know enough about history to chart a convincing etiology of what by now is a fundamental predisposition. The Industrial Revolution seems a likely candidate as the original carrier of the virus until one remembers that pre-industrial novelists created shameless heroines chatting about the size and proficiency of a man's "machine" and that pre-Common Era philosophers postulated a fine haze of rarefied particles to account for the composition of the human soul.

But what has gone out of our time is the attitude of worshipful resignation before the inconceivable and the fatal. It is quite possible that all that has happened in the course of the millennia is that we have only switched metaphors. The low level of spirituality is a historical constant. Today, for all our rhetoric about freedom, uniqueness and choice, we project ourselves as complex structural or functional units. In medieval times, people tended to see themselves as pieces of pottery, humble or magnificent, turned out by the hand of God and intended for different but predetermined uses. The milk jug was not to covet the status of the wine amphora.

On Making Love and Having Sex

The school of Behaviorism is just a modern equivalent of the old belief in predestination. Given enough time and sufficient data, human life is entirely predictable; whereas for the medieval mind man is stamped at birth with personal and social essence as if God wielded an ontological cookie-cutter: star, bell, circle. But there is a subtle discrimination to be made here. For medieval man, though human life may be predetermined, God's purposes remain eternally inscrutable. We can never know the why and the how of divine ordination. Thus the habit of obedience and reverence before the power and the mystery of the universe in which man was allowed to participate. A thread of the sacramental runs through all that brutality and ignorance we read about. We regard ourselves, however, as more enlightened than our forbears and in many ways we indisputably are; yet in assuming the paradigm of mechanism—in changing metaphors—we have forfeited our essential humanity to the illusion of indefinite perfectability. Next year's model will be better than this year's. Thus, socialism is the terminal point of human history, the perfected social structure, all its parts in eutectic sync.

Today there is no doubt that we tend compulsively to think in terms of object, function or mechanism whenever we consider the incalculably human. Love is something to be "worked at" like a problem in mathematics that must be solved for the sake of its practical application. Friendship is called a "support system." A Pascalian terror before the cold immensity of the universe is excessive "stress," as if one were absorbing too much force for the mental "structure" to distribute and resolve successfully. A novel or a poem is only the manifestation of an "abstract model." Wisdom is a kind of "flexible adaptability." Desire is libidinal "tension" which must be "discharged." And what was once called "making love," an expression that however glibly it was employed still retained the implication of a genetic mystery, is today airily dismissed as "having sex," a phrase which seems to concede in the direction of honesty but really betrays our attitude of therapeutic mechanism—like having an enema, a check-up or an operation. Sex is an excellent way of running the machine.

The cybernetic revolution has only abetted this most infectious of diseases. We not only tend to regard ourselves as biological computers but have begun to fall in love with cute little cadmium-powered robots with numbers for names and CPUs for brains. The joke is that we will have to wait until the Grade-B humanoids take over the world for the numinous and spiritual dimension of life to make its retributive comeback. At some critical point in this manganese utopia the robot will insensibly begin to consider his support system as a friend, his repair facility as a prophet, and his cell recharger as that most profound and unsearchable of mysteries, a spouse.

Cowboys and Indians, Canadian Style

Canada's Social Justice agenda did not fare well in the renegotiated NAFTA deal, rebranded as the U.S.-Mexico-Canada Agreement (USMCA). A chapter dedicated to gender rights, something Canada pushed hard for, was not incorporated into the Agreement. Trump would have no part of it. The exclusion makes good sense since special gender privileges for women, the spawn of hard-core feminism, have nothing to do with economic issues, tariffs or trade and manufacturing reciprocities.

Equally significant, a separate chapter on Indigenous Rights failed to make the cut, a serious blow to the aboriginal resistance movement which has become a rallying cry not only for Native activists but for the Canadian political, media and academic elites. These latter are committed to abrogating national jurisdictions and dismantling the historical structure of the country in a torrent of land-claim and legal negotiations favoring the so-called First Nations.

The sentimentalizing of Native history and culture has given the indigenous peoples pride of place in the Canadian imagination and in Canadian law. It has permitted radicals to wreak havoc for years in communities like Caledonia, which became a war zone, or, with the complicity of the Supreme Court, permitted indigenous activists and leaders to use treaty claims and land rights to block much-needed economic development projects. Admittedly, not all band chiefs are on board with this divisive program, and certain tribes like the Osoyoos Indian Band, a member of the Okanagan Nation Alliance, led by Chief Clarence Louie, have prospered by adopting entrepreneurial methods and practices. As Louie understood, there is more to solvency and self-reliance than casinos and cigarettes. But such instances of visionary prudence are exceptions to the general rule.

On the whole, one may be forgiven for suspecting that a shakedown operation has been in play for years. Who can forget Theresa Spence, an Attawapiskat chief of markedly portly stature who staged a hunger strike to protest the Conservative government's failure, as the CBC website put it, "to take First Nations concerns seriously.'" Reportedly nourished on a traditional fish soup diet during her ordeal, she emerged to national acclaim six weeks later as rotund as when she began her protest. But there was a fly in the ointment. As *MacLean's Magazine* reported, "the results of a damning audit into Attawapiskat's books… show[ed] the band had not properly accounted for millions of dollars in federal spending dating back to 2005."

Band chiefs and their adjuncts are notoriously prone to cooking the books and raking in exorbitant salaries. Spence's partner, Clayton Kennedy, paid $850 a day to manage the band's finances, was shortly after the hunger games charged with fraud. As the *Toronto Sun* reports, the Spence household was swimming in cash. Despite the controversy, Spence was re-elected to a new term as band chief. And indeed, notwithstanding a number of negative reports, pro-Native sentiment has not diminished much among Canada's left-leaning polity. Indian bands are generally given a pass when it comes to allegations of corruption and mismanagement.

Canada's indigenizers bear a spooky resemblance to that committee of "sappy women" in *The Adventures of Tom Sawyer* imploring the governor to be merciful to Injun Joe, "believed to have killed five citizens of the village." Many "tearful and eloquent meetings had been held" in Injun Joe's favor and there were "plenty of weaklings ready to scribble their names to a pardon-petition." Our own weaklings are sappily prepared to surrender portions of the country to aboriginal claims of sovereignty over tribal territory. Longmire in a sweat lodge is not American policy. Justin Trudeau in Theresa Spence's teepee is the Canadian way.

The delusion doesn't stop with our political elites, fellow-traveling journalists and the mass of popular sentiment. Our universities, ostensibly centers of learning and the quest for objective truth, have also lent their authority to this churning stew of nonsense, turning a feel-good fable into a scholarly farce.

More than twenty years ago, for example, the University of Saskatchewan began hiring Native professors not on the strength of academic merit or scholarly attainment but on the pleonastic grounds of "lived experience"—prompting the question of what would constitute its opposite. Dead experience? The latest campus initiative in this country, of which faculties and administrations are inordinately proud, is "indigenization" studies in which the Native peoples are regarded as peaceful and responsible stewards of the land ruthlessly oppressed by white European settlers.

That the indigenous peoples were no less ruthless in warfare and tribal exterminations and engaged in hunting practices that led to the near extinction of native species is rarely mentioned. As the Foundation for Economic Education has shown, history textbooks have been eager to promote the myth of the ecological Indian. Though European settlers were also complicit in the thinning of herds, especially the plains bison, native hunting techniques were indisputably destructive. No matter. The early inhabitants of the land are seen as pastoral angels, noble environmentalists *avant la lettre*.

The act of genuflection shows no sign of abating. Wilfrid Laurier University in Ontario, albeit a tenth-tier institution on the same level as the University of Namibia, acknowledges that it sits on the "traditional territory of the Haudenosaunee, Anishnawbe and Neutral Peoples," and has opened a Centre for Indigegogy where the visitor is fulsomely showered with coruscating greetings: Boozhoo, Wachiya, Kwe, Tansi, and She:kon. And woe betide any professor who wishes to initiate a conversation about Residential Schools, as did the unfortunate psychology professor Rick Mehta, fired despite tenure by Acadia University in Nova Scotia.

A grassroots resistance movement called Idle No More has arisen to advance the claim of aboriginal sovereignty and to "reinstitute traditional laws." Organizing protests and flash mobs, it seeks to oppose "a time when global corporate profits rule," and has jumped aboard the intersectionality bandwagon—"race, gender, sexuality, class and other identity constructions in ongoing oppression"—which will appeal to the university crowd and promote its influence in the media and political echelons. But it is based on a complete fiction, which political scientist Tom Flanagan has thoroughly debunked.

In *First Nations: Second Thoughts*, Flanagan analyzes claims of aboriginal sovereignty. Advocates of aboriginal rights believe that "Indian nations were at one time sovereign nations of equal status with European nations under international law," something that did not exist at the time. "Whether, like the Mohawks, they now aspire to sovereign statehood or, like the Assembly of First Nations, they are content to demand a share of Canadian sovereignty, they are united in thinking that their ancestors were unjustifiably deprived of the sovereignty they once possessed." In the U.S., of course, such claims are less threatening owing to the supremacy of Congress, an institution whose plenary powers the Canadian Parliament lacks. In Canada the aboriginal claim of an inherent right to self-government "is an assertion of sovereignty contrary to [our] history, jurisprudence, and national interest."

As Ricardo Duchesne points out in *Canada in Decay*, a tribe is not a nation. "The natives of Canada were organized in tribes, and a tribe consists of people with a distinct set of cultural and linguistic traits that are not yet integrated into a nation with clear boundaries and a centralized authority." The characteristics which identify a civilized state of living comprise, *inter alia*, "a written language, a legal code, a network of communications, a reasonably centralized army [and] a bureaucracy capable of enforcing state authority over an extended territory with some boundaries."

According to these criteria, the "First Nations" were not nations by any stretch of the imagination. They were a loose collection of tribal cultures. And Turtle Island, the name given by some of these tribes to the land mass we call North America, is not a country but a vague geographical designation or part of a Creation story. The presumed national status of the indigenous inhabitants is a sentimental myth invented by native proponents of sovereign rights and privileges and by a guilt-ridden people—good Canadians—wedded to the canard of "Social Justice" and to the liberal ideology of anti-colonialism.

Flanagan concludes his volume by suggesting that improvement in the lot of the Native peoples—who in some respects enjoy more than equal status than their fellow citizens, including, as the Indian Act stipulates, reserve-based tax exemption—will not depend on a web of complex and draining negotiations that disrupt the conduct of Canada's affairs. Rather, independent and entrepreneurial activity on the part of individuals and enlightened band chiefs, as noted with respect to the Osoyoos Indian Band, is the sine qua non for Native development, prosperity and dignity. Individuals and tribes must take responsibility for their lives rather than rely on vociferous and parasitical demands for historical restitution and an endless tangle of legal ratifications.

Perhaps all is not lost. Sometimes one comes across refreshing instances of cultural sanity. Chief Clarence Louie is a far-sighted leader. And I think of my friend Neil Gabriel, a self-employed tradesman and ancestral Mohawk from the Kanesatake Reserve in Oka, Quebec, who was humorously skeptical of the claims, exemptions and romanticizings surrounding the Native populations. "If we want to know what kind of winter we can expect," he once joked, "we look at the white man's woodpile."

Is Islam a Religion?

The status of Islam should be clarified if the debate on how to defeat terrorism is ever to bear fruit. Islam, I would argue, is not a religion in the common acceptation of the term as a community of believers dedicated to the loving worship of the Divine, the sanctity of life, and the institution of moral principles governing repentance for sins and crimes, making life on earth a stage toward a higher reincarnation, an ineffable peace, or a confirmatory prelude to eternity in the realm of a righteous and merciful God.

In fact, Islam is an unrepentant politico-expansionist movement clothed in the trappings of religion and bent on universal conquest by whatever means it can mobilize: deception (*taqiyya*), social and cultural infiltration, or bloody violence, as its millennial history and authoritative scriptures have proven. (See Koran 13:41, which is meant literally despite the attempt of apologists to launder its purport: "Do they not see that We are advancing in the land, diminishing it by its borders on all sides?")

There are several ways in which Islam differs from all other major religions. For starters:

- It sanctions militant proselytization, mandating forcible imposition on other peoples by coercion, threat and overt violence (Koran 8:39, 9:29, etc.), a practice unique among religions today.

- It punishes apostasy with death (Koran 4:89; Hadith, Bukhari 9.84.57), also a practice unique among religions today.

- It countenances no separation between church and state, that is, it cannot render unto Caesar what is Caesar's, since it *is* Caesar.

The scope of its ambition is *khilafil*, that is, the establishment of a Caliphate requiring that a state—ultimately a universal state—be ruled by Islamic law. As Muslim scholar Jaafar Sheikh Idris explains, "Secularism cannot be a solution for countries with a Muslim majority or even a sizeable minority, for it requires people to replace their God-given beliefs with an entirely different set of man-made beliefs. Separation of religion and state is not an option for Muslims because it requires us to abandon Allah's decree for that of man."

- The "religion" itself takes precedence over the transcendent values it should strive to attain: the flourishing of the individual soul, the love of God's Creation, the grace and miracle of life, the conversation with the Divine, freedom of conscience and the inviolability of personal choice in determining one's redemption. Instead, it elevates conformity to a set of stringent rules, down to the smallest detail, as a prerequisite to salvation, whose effect is primarily to perpetuate the faith itself at the expense of the individual votary. Admittedly, this is a literalist practice common to most restrictive and comparatively minor orthodoxies, but regarding the massive following enjoyed by Islam and its susceptibility to violence and the subjugation of other faiths and peoples to its hegemony, we are remarking a radically greater economy of scale and the havoc it can wreak.

- The propensity to violence is not an aberration but an intrinsic element of the Islamic corpus. The much-bruited notion that there is such a thing as "Islamism," a form of extremism that has nothing to do with Islam proper, or is a perversion thereof, is a pure canard, another in a series of timorous progressivist memes bleaching the blood out of the Islamic ideological *jalabiyya*. Islam, not "Islamism," promises paradise for martyrs and jihadis killed in battle (Koran 3: 157), thus palliating and even inciting feral attitudes and fanatical actions—a patently non-spiritual way of earning beatitude.

- As Howard Kainz points out in an illuminating essay, "Islam and the Decalogue," Islam reverses the Golden Rule, which is central to Judaism, Christianity, Hinduism, Buddhism and Confucianism (Koran 48:29, 2:191, 3:28, etc.). For this reason, Kainz concludes,

> "Islam may best be understood," not as a religion, but "as a worldwide cult."

The standard rebuttal that all faiths have at one time or another shown themselves prone to violence and repression misses the essential point. All the major religions have reformed themselves, reducing or eliminating the all-too-human tendency to sanctimonious oppression—and none of these faiths, let us remember, endorsed oppression as a *universal* creedal or Divine imperative. Such is not the case with Islam, a communion that since its inception in the 7th Century has seldom strayed from its sanguinary path of carnage and subdual. Its incendiary prescriptions and commands, as many scholars have noted, are open-ended and contain no "sunset clause." They are perpetual and mandatory.

Others might argue that world-historical numbers are sufficient to constitute the legitimacy of a belief system. An *ummah* comprising a billion-and-a-half adherents is no trifling matter. Numbers, however, do not in themselves determine what qualifies as an ethically reputable, socially harmonious or spiritually viable religion or political grouping. Nazism and Communism counted millions of devout believers, but no reasonable person would consider such covenants as morally justifiable. Not coincidentally, both of these totalitarian movements found a natural home in Islam: Communism in the pan-Arab nationalist and Nazism in a canonical Islam already richly manured with anti-Semitic beliefs and tropes. With respect to the latter, we recall the Grand Mufti of Jerusalem Haj Amin al-Husseini's's infamous collaboration with Hitler to further the aims of the Axis powers and facilitate the Nazi "final solution" of the "Jewish question." Islam plainly shares the same septicemic tendencies and imperial ambitions as its two erstwhile political allies, as it does their popular appeal.

Islam is, consequently, not a "religion of peace," as our weak-minded and complicit "leaders"—politicians, intellectuals, academics and journalists—tirelessly and tiresomely claim. "Islam is not terrorizing the West because it *can*," writes Raymond Ibrahim, "but because it is being *allowed* to"—legally as well as sentimentally, we might add.

In the name of avoiding so-called slanderous stereotypes and of promoting "diversity," the powers-that-be refuse to recognize that Islam is, in effect, a triumphalist political theology of conquest and colonial subordination wherever and whenever it manifests itself, and has shown itself to be largely immune to doctrinal retrofitting.

Many observers object that measures intended to check the depredations of Islam violate the provisions of the First Amendment. Among the freedoms it guarantees, the First Amendment specifies that "Congress shall make no law respecting an establishment of religion, or prohibiting the free exercise thereof." If, these skeptics fear, one creates an exception to the Constitution and allows the government to certify what clerics are permitted to preach, such an intervention could be misused in the future against any person or institution the authorities deem unacceptable. This caveat must be acknowledged and taken into consideration, but, as we will see in the ensuing, the issue is not as definitive as it might initially appear.

Rebecca Bynum, publisher and managing editor of *New English Review*, has brilliantly analyzed the doctrinal nature of Islam in connection with the extent and the limits of the First Amendment in her masterful 2011 study *Allah Is Dead: Why Islam Is Not a Religion*. The book is a must-read for anyone interested in examining the theological-and-political orientation of Islam, in particular for anyone who is unclear or apprehensive about the legislative purview of the First Amendment. The fundamental questions Bynum addresses are whether or not Islam "should rightly be classified as a religion, let alone an 'Abrahamic religion' or one of the 'world's great religions,'" and whether or not the Constitution protects freedom of religion "but only within certain bounds."

An important precedent, she continues, involved the status of polygamy in the Mormon faith, a usage rejected by the federal government, which threatened Utah with military invasion unless it repudiated the practice, the Supreme Court having ruled in 1878 that it is not just to tolerate polygamy in the name of religious freedom. The ruling read, in part: "The government cannot make laws regarding religion, but can reach actions when the principles are a violation of social duties or subversive of good order.". The state complied, officially banning polygamy in the territory. As a result, Bynum writes, "[T]he Mormon Church now has protection under the religious liberty clause, but it did not while…its members practiced polygamy." Curiously, although polygamy is permitted in Islam (Koran 4:3, Bukhari 62.2,6), the government has not moved to prohibit it among its Muslim citizens as a violation of moral and religious principle. What's not good for Mormonism is apparently good for Islam, the historic interpretation of the First Amendment be damned.

The Founders, Bynum asserts, "clearly meant to define religion in a Judeo-Christian context." Islam, however, "is self-segregating, fosters ideas of Muslim supremacy and thereby sows seeds of social discord." What kind of religion, we might ask, degrades women as second-class citizens, approves anti-Semitism, preaches hatred against "infidels," sponsors terrorist attacks on an almost daily basis with Koranic warrant, and wishes to impose Sharia, "a parallel legal system based on inequality," on its Western host countries?

Furthermore, as we have seen, Islam insists on territorial sovereignty and does not distinguish between theology and politics, which is why its definitional status as a "religion" is or should be moot. Its rituals, edicts, directives and precepts impact culture, politics and society as a whole on both the macro and micro levels. Bynum gets to the heart of the matter: "If Islam continues to be classified as a religion and given the full protection and benefits religions receive in America, then we will be helpless to contain it."

"Free societies," observes Bret Stephens in *The Wall Street Journal*, articulating a historically validated truism, "cannot survive through progressive accommodations to barbarians." In the same vein, Ibrahim alludes to the statistical reality of Islam's "rule of Numbers," which refers not to the world-wide Islamic census, but to the rise of violence proportionate to Muslim immigration figures: "The more Muslims grow in numbers, the more Islamic phenomena intrinsic to the Muslim world—in this case, brazen violence against 'infidels'—appear."

I would therefore agree with Bynum that, as historically and scripturally constituted, Islam is not entitled to the protectionist provisions of the First Amendment. Its exclusion would solve the problem of potential abuse of the Amendment's terms and stipulations. Islam's tenets and articles of belief, undeniably unjust, tyrannical and socially disruptive in their practical effects and moral implications, should be construed constitutionally inadmissible, in line with the determination of the Supreme Court in its 1878 decision. Indeed, the issue is far graver today than it was a century and a half ago.

Bynum's final chapter furnishes a compendious list of categories that define the true nature of religion, and makes it clear that Islam does not pass muster. As she summarizes, "Just because Muslims are convinced Islam is a religious faith, doesn't mean the rest of us have to accept it as such under our laws, laws that were meant to foster religions that exalt value, advance morality, nurture the individual, preserve wisdom, promote peace, strengthen the family and have a transcendent purpose." I can't but assume that Chief Justice Waite, who delivered the opinion of the 1878 court, would have concurred.

The spiritual nature and moral vision of Islam are antithetical to both the idea and the ideal of a genuine religious communion. On the contrary, its drive and aspiration are *khilafil*. As a result, I believe it is fair to say that Islam is a theological-political hybrid intent on domination—the conversion, taxing (*jizzya*) or annihilation—of the non-Muslim world, defined in Islam as the *Dar-al-Harb* (House or Land of War). It's there in the holy books for anyone to read. It's there in the muezzin's *adhan* (call to prayer), exhortations from the *minbar* (pulpit in a mosque) and the *khutbah* (Islamic sermons) for anyone to hear. It's there in the diktats of the *ulema* for anyone with the stamina to comb the literature to find. It's there in the historical annals for anyone to study. It's there among the bodies of the murdered and the mutilated for anyone, who has the stomach for it, to witness.

To conclude. Adopting the words of the 1878 Supreme Court judgment, the "principles" of Islam are a violation of "social duties and good order." As such, Islam does not merit the legal shelter of the

First Amendment. Measures to limit its influence—a halt to unvetted immigration, restrictions on subversive preaching, dead-bolting dissident mosques, de-licensing inflammatory imams, prohibiting the establishment of No-Go Zones, invigilating Muslim schools, preventing Muslim conversion tactics in prisons, and decreeing Sharia in contravention of common law and incompatible with pluralistic Western democracies—are fully justified.

We can be sure that as things now stand the Democratic Party (like the Liberal Party in my own country) will do nothing of significance to combat the growing demographic weight of Islam and the terror that flows from it—as *National Post* columnist Rex Murphy says, "The attacks come at such speed…[w]e need a terror spreadsheet"—but will continue to cater to the Muslim voting bloc while engineering the collapse of the classical liberal traditions that have guaranteed our freedoms and prosperity. Progressivism and Islam go hand in hand—until, that is, the day when Islam is strong enough to destroy its collaborator. Refusing to meaningfully resist the Muslim incursion into the body social can lead only to the formation of a dhimmified culture, at which point it may be too late to reclaim our patrimony. Islam is a civilizational enemy that has no business claiming asylum under the aegis of the First Amendment and our political establishment has no business giving Islam a constitutional waiver. If Pope Francis is correct when he proclaims that "Religions don't want war," then Islam is not a religion.

Commenting on the Danish People's Party's call to shut down Muslim immigration, *American Thinker* editor Thomas Lifson writes "As the West grapples with the threat of violent jihad, I suspect we will be seeing more consideration of whether Islam is merely a religion or rather a totalitarian political doctrine." Let's hope he's right.

The Angel of History

Nothing is too big to fail, including civilizations, and ours is no exception. The decline of the West is historically inevitable. The agencies by which civilizational atrophy and degeneration work are readily isolated: the endemic vices and pathologies of human nature (greed, resentment, hatred, envy, sloth); the tendency to take for granted the benefits, rights and privileges that have been painfully won in the past and gradually squandered in the present; the eclipse of historical memory and the concomitant exhaustion of mental vigilance. Whether decline can be retarded is, of course, an open question, but one thing is certain: pushback is futile absent the recognition of the symptoms of decay.

Perhaps the most evident sign of civilizational devolution is the inability or unwillingness to acknowledge reality, to come to terms with things as they are, and to oppose the suppression of objectivity and its substitution by fantasy, illusion and wish-fulfillment. The resonating dictum of the pre-Socratic Greek philosopher Parmenides from his fragmentary poem *On Nature*—variously translated as *what is, is, and what is not, is not!*—sounds like an empty tautology. But it has relevance for our present historical moment, with respect to the cultural and lexical inversions of contemporary thought and discourse. Apart from its metaphysical implications, which we won't go into here, the Parmenidean maxim expresses the criterion for survival, the need to separate truth (*aletheia*) from opinion (*doxa*) and to recognize things as they are if an individual, a culture, or a people is to transact successfully with the existing world. But when thought and action come to be governed by the anarchic principle that *what is, is not and what is not, is*, a process of social, political and epistemological disintegration invariably sets in. This is the condition in which the West finds itself today.

Notes from a Derelict Culture

At every turn, the real is conceptually abolished by a cult-like mindset that vitiates the social and cultural life of a people by performing, as David Mamet points out in *The Secret Knowledge*, an act of sacrifice on the altar of superstition and willed ignorance. The new observances, he writes, "must absolutely repudiate the old," a form of disavowal especially typical of the Left which is in the process "of sacrificing production, exploitation of natural resources and an increasing standard of living" in order to propitiate its gods and ensure the preservation of a global hallucination, a pervasive climate of *doxa*.

It is as if the Soviet pseudo-scientist Trofim Lysenko has risen from the grave and, by a mordant historical irony, infected not the burgeoning Russian empire but a weak and decadent West that has succumbed to a sterile and perilous sort of intellectual vernalization—a term glibly misused by Lysenko to describe the process, mistakenly thought heritable, of forcing winter cereals to behave like spring cereals. As plant biologist Richard Amasino writes, Lysenko's belief that vernalized transformations could be inherited "fit the Marxist ideology that…a Marxist society could produce heritable changes in attitude, and, thus, if the proper environment was provided, future generations would consist of improved citizens. Lysenko's efforts," he continues, "to obtain or fabricate results that supported a political ideology…had disastrous consequences for Russian genetics." Where the speculative and the real are in flagrant contradiction, the results are almost always catastrophic.

The West is now busy at work across the entire field of social, cultural and political life promoting its own version of Lysenkoism, a misconceived exercise of supposedly vernalizing reality by transforming fact into fantasy and truth into lie for the purpose of creating the perfect society and the redeemed human being, transferable across the generations. Its assumptions about the world are guided not by common sense or genuine science but by the precepts of ideology and political desire.

Examples abound of the ubiquitous tendency to replace ontology with myth, the determinate with the fluid and the objective with the delusionary. A modest inventory of such noxious miscontruals would include:

- Biological sexual differentiation must yield to voluntary gender identity.
- A cooling climate is obviously warming.
- The demonstrable failure of socialism wherever it has been tried is proof that it has not been properly implemented.
- Democratic Israel is an apartheid state.
- Islam with its record of unstinting bloodshed is a religion of peace.
- Illegal immigrants are undocumented workers.
- Terrorism is workplace violence.
- A child in the womb is a mass of insensible protoplasm.
- The killing of the old and the ill is merciful, even when the recipient of such tender concern is not consulted.
- There is no such thing as truth, an axiom regarded as true.
- Green energy is a social and economic good irrespective of crony profiteering, exorbitant cost, wildlife devastation, and unworkability in its present state.
- Storms, earthquakes, volcanic eruptions, floods, tsunamis and mortality itself are natural phenomena, but Nature, which cares nothing for human life, is nonetheless sacred, vulnerable and at the mercy of human indifference.
- Women are disadvantaged in the workforce, academia and society at large despite the fact that high-end hiring practices, legal judgments, custody protocols and university appointments, as well as student enrollment, wholly favor women to the detriment of men.
- An enemy is a friend.
- Criminality is innocence.
- Losing is winning.
- Prosperity is avarice.
- Redistributing wealth, i.e., robbing the affluent and productive, is a form of compassion and basic justice.
- Those who claim victim status are always credible.
- Accumulating debt is an economic stimulus.

- Big government is a boon to mankind.
- War is *passé* (so 19th century).
- Diplomacy and talk—the higher Twitter—will prevail over barbarism.
- The most gynocentric society ever created is a rape culture.
- Palestine is a historically legitimate nation.
- Uniformity of thought and action equals cultural diversity.
- An exploded lie merely confirms what it lies about (e.g., Rigoberta Menchu).
- Morality is relative.
- Merit is an unearned distinction.

Or in other words, what is, is not, and what is not, is.

Let us hope that sociologist Emile Durkhein was right when he wrote: "There is a limit to the quota of abnormality which the collective mind (the public) is capable of perceiving." But the prospects are not encouraging. This species of Orwellian inversion, supplanting the real by the imaginary, is now an intrinsic component of the Western psyche and firmly embedded in what French thinker Pierre Bourdieu in his influential treatise *Distinction* calls the social *habitus*— a system of norms, usages, taboos and conventions that steer thought and behavior in certain approved directions and from which individuals should strive to emancipate themselves. Of course, Bourdieu's notion of "social emancipation" remains solidly in the camp of Leftist mischief and he would likely approve of the "misrecognitions" (his term) listed above. The current *habitus* is most conspicuous in the repressive operations of political correctness and the canard of "social justice."

The celebrated 1920 print *Angelus Novus* by Paul Klee, now in the collection of the Israel Museum in Jerusalem, foretells and encapsulates the degradation of Western civilization. The work represents a premonitory and grieving angel blown by the winds of Time backward into the future while gazing upon the detritus of the present and the past. In the words of philosopher and critical theorist Walter Benjamin's

The Angel of History

Angelus Novus by Paul Klee

Theses on the Philosophy of History from *Illuminations*: "This is how one pictures the angel of history...Where we perceive a chain of events, he sees one single catastrophe that keeps piling ruin upon ruin and hurls it in front of his feet. The angel would like to stay, awaken the dead, and make whole what has been smashed. But a storm is blowing from Paradise; it has got caught in his wings with such violence that the angel can no longer close them. The storm irresistibly propels him into the future to which his back is turned, while the pile of debris before him grows skyward. This storm is what we call progress." Or, rather than "progress," in the sulphurous light of ongoing Western dereliction, one might more aptly say "progressivism."

When a civilization, or its cultural and intellectual curators who wield the instruments of power and authority, re-interprets reality as merely discretionary, decline and eventual extinction are guaranteed, and the Angel of History will preside over the ruins. When pretending becomes believing, and believing becomes mandatory, and calling out the naked emperor is punishable by law or fine or ostracism or loss of employment or worse, and when the scale of such abuses becomes effectively global, the "lifeworld," or communal nature of daily life, as we have known it has ceased to exist.

Biology, Nature, economic forces and human nature are not disposable artifacts, fashion accessories or hypothetical creations of unanchored will. They can be investigated, plumbed, to some limited degree modified and harnessed to advantage, but they cannot be turned into something they are not or conveniently abolished without unleashing tragic consequences. As Ludwig Wittgenstein disarmingly put it in his *Tractatus Logico-Philosophicus*, channelling Parmenides, "The world is whatever is the case" and "the totality of facts determines what is the case, and also whatever is not the case." The implication is that reality is an unforgiving taskmaster. It is oblivious of civilized — and indeed, human — life, despite the confidence of those for whom reality is only a "social construct" (or in updated jargon, "socially determined") or a pliant servant of ideological conviction. Such hubris exacts its price and it is one we cannot afford to pay.

The only sensible response to the collapse we are experiencing is probably terminal depression. Yet what choice do we have but to persist in trying to beat back the flood of cultural desuetude and personal despair, as at the end of Samuel Beckett's novel *The Unnamable*:

> *You must go on.*
> *I can't go on.*
> *I'll go on.*

Notwithstanding, perhaps in the long run the only way to beat the cultural odds is to let the culture crash of its own accord, as it most likely will, and hope against hope that a viable replacement, a new and better form of civilized life, will rise Phoenix-like from the ashes. Perhaps then the angel of history will fly forward.

The New Puritans

One of the primary foci of the current cultural zeitgeist features the preoccupation, mounting to an obsession, with one or another form of sex, the more aberrant the better—the phobic obsession with rape, sympathetic coverage of re-assignment surgery and body modification, injunctions against deadnaming and heteronormativity, the emphasis on cisgender guilt, the sanctifying of gay marriage, the injustices of something called the "patriarchy," the explosion of sexual harassment charges against media and political celebrities, the emphasis on sexualising criminal justice proceedings in favor of women (aka gender disparity), and even legal bestiality. Moreover, the biological division between man and woman has been re-conceived as a "social construct" that must be unlearned, the product of a vast priapic conspiracy.

The feverish obsession with sex in all its myriad forms and embodiments has led to some very bizarre ideas and mind-numbing outcomes, of which gender (or non-biological) self-identification and transgender fluidity are among the most conspicuous. The pursuit of the sexual makeover has become gruesomely popular. And when mother and son transition to father and daughter, we know we have entered the twilight zone. Indeed, one feels as if one is living among James Cameron's epicene avatars or deep in some psychotic's substitute world. And yet the gender radicals are chiefly accredited academics, journal editors, published feminists and government functionaries, an infallible sign that our so-called elites have entered the realm of the fabular, dragging the wider culture and its political masters with them.

What we are observing is a bizarre form of Puritanism. The visceral yet falsely denied fixation on sexual expression and behavior that we associate with the Puritan sensibility, especially as it manifested in the

Salem witch trials, has morphed into its opposite, namely, a lubricious fixation that has become publicly endorsed and applauded. The gender mavens of our time are as prurient as the witch hunters of old.

They are the Puritans of the modern age who see sex under every stone while at the same time unleashing a campaign against all that is normal and fruitful in the relation between men and women. The delusion in which they have invested—that sex and gender are conceptually unrelated and the latter trumps the former—is not only an affront to common sense but leads by unrelenting increments to the displacement of the usages and conventions on which normative life and societal flourishing depend.

A typical example of this costly absurdity is furnished by a new NIH (National Institutes of Health) study conducted by one Ethan Cicero, a post-doctoral, self-declared anti-Trump student at Duke University. Cicero (not to be confused with his noble namesake) defines "transgender" as an "umbrella term that includes a spectrum of gender identities and persons with gender expressions," entailing but not limited to "genderqueer, genderfluid, transsexual, gender nonconforming, and two-spirit people." Gender, he argues, is more "abstract" than sex, referring to "the complex relationships among gender biology (sex), gender identity (one's sense of being female, male, both, or neither), and gender expression (outward presentation behaviours, and roles)."

"Abstract" is probably the wrong word; Cicero surely meant "comprehensive." In any event, biological sex is a mere discursive starting point and counts for little in the colourful pageant of sexual identities marching down cultural Main Street. Gender Pride takes precedence over common life, denouncing and shaming all that is healthy and proven in the very bedrock of human history. Nature is just not that malleable, but nature never stopped a gender Puritan.

Gender fanaticism has gone viral, infecting every corner of life: language, marriage, genuine social reciprocity, freedom of thought and expression, and the productive and symbiotic relation to reality.

Individuals are encouraged to *look within* to find where on the vast continuum of gender possibilities they might fit. Meanwhile the heterosexual male mainstream is under attack for the crime of harboring a normal sexual drive, believing in romance and wishing to start a family. It is no accident that the feminist left has seen fit to ridicule Vice-President Mike Pence as a strictly traditional monogamist.

The new Puritanism cannot abide the time-tested sanctities and moral underpinnings of the Western tradition, in particular with regard to the institution of marriage, durable relationships, or the productive biologically based "contract" that allows for the perpetuation of normative civic existence. The new Puritanism is a pietistic fraud that puts sexual experimentation and violations of the norm before the stable arrangements that promote social and cultural continuity. The Mike Pences of this world must be pilloried and excommunicated while the Caitlyn Jenners are to be celebrated and canonized.

Absent bacterial cell division, the genetic binary is a fact of nature and those who propose that sexual dimorphism is a "social construct" that must be undone are flirting not only with one another but with disaster. The irony of this latest development, however, has escaped its progenitors, for it is precisely the trans phenomenon that is a "social construct." It does not exist in nature; it has been invented. As my wife Janice Fiamengo writes in an article titled *Is Feminism a Religion*, "If evidence for the biological basis of sex is brought forward, a feminist will simply claim in response that all science is sexist," in other words, we are sexist if we do not consider sex and multiple forms of sexual identity, however anomalous, as the end-all and be-all of human striving rather than as merely one aspect of mutual existence. It may be said that the Puritans of old suffered from repression and projection. The new Puritans suffer from genderitis, that is, libidinous self-election.

When culture attempts to pre-empt nature and deny biology, the result is catastrophic: the disintegration of civil existence, illusion substituting for reality and the peripheral displacing the central. Meanwhile, pressing issues on which our prosperity and survival depend—a precarious economy, domestic subversion, Islamic jihad, unvetted and illegal immigration, international conflict, the falling replacement fertility rate—go unattended. Buying into a subprime version of reality can lead to only one result: the foreclosing of the cultural mortgage. No matter. The gender Puritans go marching on.

Utopia: Good Place or No Place?

The Golden Age - Lucas Cranach the Elder. c1530

Much has been written about the perennial temptation of the Utopian project embraced by intellectuals and political reformers across the ages. The impulse to radically transform existent society and replace it with a new, smoothly functioning, and presumably idyllic alternative never seems to diminish, a sign of perpetual dissatisfaction with the world as it is and, to a great and unchangeable extent, must be. The subject is as timely as it is timeless and slides along a continuum between the nostalgic desire for what once was or might have been and the revolutionary ambition to create a social paradise in the here and now.

As to be expected, the literature is interminable, grouped for the most part under the generic term "Utopian fiction" and including a wide ambit of texts of considerable thematic latitude, ranging from the Garden of Gems in the ninth tablet of *The Epic of Gilgamesh*, the Garden of Eden in *Genesis* and the Golden Age in Hesiod's *Works and Days* (when men "dwelt in ease and peace") to, say, Edward Bellamy's *Looking Backward*, B.F. Skinner's *Walden Two* and Ernest Callenbach's *Ecotopia*. The models developed are practically countless and, in the later exemplars, the rhapsody of destruction masking as beneficent change pretty well uncontrollable.

The myth of the earthly paradise or Golden Age has taken many forms, for example, the belief in an El Dorado hidden deep in inaccessible jungles, which animated explorers of old and was mercilessly mocked in Voltaire's *Candide*; or the construction of an entirely new organization of social and political life, the attempt to bring the Golden Age into time, whether by stealth or by force. But perhaps the most celebrated source for the concept of Utopia, among a plethora of classical and Renaissance works too numerous to mention here, is Thomas More's 1516 treatise of that name. More's *Utopia* fixed the word in the language and is often read as a serious exploration of a possible, rationally conceived society, that is, of an "eu-topos," the Greek word for "good place." At the very least it reified the dream that has never ceased to beckon. The problem with this benign interpretation is that it dismisses the many satirical or ambifocal elements that call the book's ostensible thesis into question.

It's worth looking closely at More's seminal book, which "deconstructs" the *beau idéal* of the Utopian program, revealing all sorts of deflationary traces that appear to signal More's original intent. Scholarship has determined that *Utopia* owes much to Lucian's *True History*, which More had earlier translated, in which the 2nd century satirist had rollicking fun at the expense of the idea of another world categorically better than the one we inhabit. Names and titles are an even more direct giveaway. As Paul Turner points out in his introduction to the Penguin edition of *Utopia*, the main character's surname, Hythlodaeus, is Greek for "dispenser of folly" or "Nonsenso." The title of "chief magistrate," Ademus, means "peopleless," the river Anydras is "no water" and, of course, "Utopia" in its first acceptation is "ou-topos" or "no place."

It gets even better as we move along. None of the inhabitants of Utopia, apart from Hythlodaeus, are given personal names, for they are not real people. The Utopians find Lucian "delightfully entertaining," oblivious to the fact that he judged their progenitors a pack of utter imbeciles. Utopia has passed sumptuary laws forbidding extravagance in dress and accoutrement, yet exports "scarlet and purple cloth" to advance trade. The heads of family units are called "syphogrants" (silly old men) and their superiors are known as "tranibors" (plain gluttons). The capital of Utopia is Amaurotum, or "Dream-town." Travel is restricted; nevertheless, the Utopians consider that "perfect happiness implies complete freedom of movement." They despise precious metals and regard ascetic acts as ludicrous, yet More himself wore a golden chain over a hair shirt. Utopians have few laws and despise lawyers, but More devoted his life to the law and became England's chief law officer. Divorce is permitted in Utopia; More went to prison rather than consent to King Henry's divorce.

Hythlodaeus asserts that private property and material accumulation are the root of evil and must be abolished. He is rebutted by the More character in the story who, clearly parsing his mentor Aristotle's *Politics*—we recall that he donates "even more of Aristotle" than of Plato to the Utopian library—argues that redistribution would lead to laziness and reduced production. Hytholodaeus has no riposte except to say that "in Utopia the facts speak for themselves," which is palpably no answer at all. Indeed, More might be described as a proto-capitalist. In his more sober tracts, he savagely attacked the ethos of communal sharing practiced by the Anabaptists, and began writing *Utopia* when he was on an embassy to Flanders to promote the wool trade and thus increase the wealth of England's mercantile classes. He was, unlike the Western progressivists of today, no redistributionist.

The list of discrepancies in the text, and the contradictions between the historical More and his fictional stand-in, would fill several pages. I've provided only the merest hint of the discontinuities that strongly suggest, despite a few scattered indications for the improvement of social life, that *Utopia* is not to be taken seriously and that it is, ultimately, a bucolic and whimsical exercise in a genre we might call "romantic satire," puncturing the figment of a surrogate Creation. *Utopia* is to be taken *cum grano*. It's also interesting to note that the book has generated a respectable posterity. One thinks in particular of Shakespeare's *The Tempest* in which a foolish Gonzalo boasts that he "would in such perfection govern [as] to excel the golden age," of Samuel Johnson's *Rasselas*, in which the Utopian world culminates in ennui and discontent, and Samuel Butler's hilarious *Erewhon* (an anagram for "Nowhere"), where everything is done backwards.

What is true of the *Utopia* and its successors is even truer of the Utopian enterprise itself, in all its diverse manifestations. It is like a country without an invoicing currency. It is riddled with incongruities and plain impossibilities, flies in the face of human nature and leads inevitably to terrible suffering. The "Big Brother" syndrome is unavoidable—as More writes, "everyone has his eyes on you." (This is a remark to be taken both literally and prophetically. Anna Funder shows in *Stasiland*, the declassified East German Stasi files revealed, as in Hitler's Germany and Stalin's USSR, a vast network of child and spousal informers spying and reporting on their own kin.)

Dystopian fictions like Orwell's *1984*, Huxley's *Brave New World*, Yvegeny Zamyatin's *We* and John Calvin Batchelor's undeservedly forgotten *The Birth of the People's Republic of Antarctica* (among others) flesh out the darker implications we find in More's *libellus* (or "little book," as he called it) and are mirrored in actual human societies that have followed the Utopian leveling and redistributive script: Soviet Russia, Mao's China, the Jongleurs' North Korea, Pol Pot's Cambodia, Mugabe's Zimbabwe, or Chavez/Maduro's Venezuela.

It's only fair to mention that Mario Vargas Llosa's magisterial novel, *The War of the End of the World*, which tells the tragic story of the 19th century Brazilian commune of Canudos, is neither dystopian nor utopian. If we want to get a bit fancy, we might call it a meso-utopian fiction, falling somewhere in between the two genres. The historical Canudos, a society of the dispossessed, seemed to work for a time, before it was destroyed by the Brazilian government. Whether a colony without money, private property or marriage, comprising the wretched of the earth under the leadership of an "apocalyptic prophet," would have flourished indefinitely is a question Llosa does not try to answer. Aside from a less turbulent microcosm of social change like Calvin's 16th century Reformation Geneva, the fate of other such real-world communities would suggest not.

We need to keep in mind that entities like Geneva or Canudos were really small, relatively homogeneous city-states, not nations occupying a different scale of magnitude. The same is true of another famous historical instance, the 17th century English Diggers' attempt to practice "the levelling of all estates" in various places around the countryside. Christopher Hill in his *The World Turned Upside Down* (a title appropriated by Melanie Phillips), sympathetically tracks the fate of this "utopian communistic society," which may or may not have survived before it was broken up by the Council of State. Another such visionary adventure, Robert Owens' New Harmony, disintegrated of its own accord. Owens' effort to inaugurate a "New Moral World" as a prelude to the millennium in which social classes and personal wealth would melt away lasted less than three years.

But on the whole, such municipal anomalies are comparatively malleable. With the possible exception of Mustafa Kemal Atatürk's Turkey, now undergoing a fresh tremblor, it amounts to a near certainty that the program envisaging the "fundamental transformation" of any large and complex society must invariably produce a *fundamental distortion* of human potentialities, impoverish its supposed beneficiaries and install in power a privileged and despotic ruling class which represents the violent antithesis of its hypothetically sacred canons. Eight years of the Obama administration make this political and economic deformation painfully clear, as does the more recent and imbecilic Green New Deal championed by Democrat congresswoman Alexandria Ocasio-Cortez.

Here it is important to recognize that the American experiment in republican governance is by no means a Utopian project, as hostile revisionists may be disposed to argue or as some Utopian speculators, claiming precedent or superior knowledge, may allege in order to bolster their ongoing efforts to remake the country. Were they to have their way, as Mike McDaniel shows in a PJM article, law would then become a function of an elastic "values"-based mission, unfinished and open-ended, subject to constant re-interpretation in the quest to construct the perfect society, at the expense of a stable social and juridical order. This is, in essence, the "living Constitution" thesis so beloved of activist judges, intellectual meliorists and "progressive" politicians. It is part of the Utopian endeavor.

But the motto *Novus ordo seclorum* (New Order of the Ages), which derives from Virgil's Fourth Eclogue and appears on the exergue of the Great Seal of the United States, obviously does not signify a Utopian upheaval. Rather, as explained by the Seal's designer Charles Thomson in 1782, the phrase purports "the beginning of the new American Era," based on profoundly moral and common sense principles. The American "New Order" is not a top-down political structure, but one that establishes the authority of the people over its legislators and representatives. Thus, the American system may be justly described as resolutely anti-Utopian, as if the Founders intuitively understood, unlike our current "experts," that chronic social bricolage is a kind of pathology and that the Elysian passion is anathema to human welfare.

And the Elysian passion is cheaply bought. An analogous idea is expressed by Eva Hoffman in her memoir *Lost in Translation* where, borrowing Alan Tate's word, she speculates that many American intellectuals and academics, primarily on the left, suffer from a form of "angelism"—"a desire to be more immaculate beings, avatars of pure ideas…so they can ricochet from one vision of utopia to another." In particular, the academic branch of the compact may seem harmless enough, like mall Santas with tenure, but the influence they wield in the education of young minds, the conduct of public discourse and the production of left-wing intellectual unanimity is highly injurious. The fact is that the Utopian predisposition unfailingly releases its own devastating contradictions, starting in the penthouse and collapsing in the basement. It cannot help but fail since it is an a priori, intellectual concept divorced from real experience, springing like Athena from the forehead of Zeus and so violating the natural process of gestation.

Utopia: Good Place or No Place

These grimly earnest seekers after social beatitude must inevitably meet, not with success but, in the words of Edgar Allen Poe, with their own shadow, the ominous side of their putative errand of light. As Poe tells it in a wise and prescient poem, *Eldorado*, such "gallant knights" at the end of their journey will only have encountered the "Shadow" and found

> *No spot of ground*
> *That looked like Eldorado.*

In the final analysis, the Utopian obsession is the kind of infantile fantasy that drives the doctrinaire socialists (and multicultural appeasers) of the day. They are the child-soldiers of the millennium who brandish grown-up weapons and are determined to bring the City of the Sun, the New Atlantis, Utopia, Arcadia, the Land of Cockaigne, the "levelling of all estates," the Golden Age of Man, the "New Moral World," Marx's "scientific socialism" or "communism," neo-Marxism, neo-Socialism, social democracy, the caring society, the welfare state, "hope and change"—call it what you will—into being by every means at their disposal. Indifferent to what More called "the grand absurdity on which [such a] society was erected," they opt for radical metamorphosis instead of gradual amelioration. They are ready, as the Russian philosopher Nicolai Berdyaev warned in *The Destiny of Man*, to sacrifice freedom for the illusion of perfection. They will turn the world upside down for our supposed benefit. It is, quite literally, a perennial ecstasis.

America especially must remain alert under politicians pledged to alter its constitutional foundations in the direction of a socialist patriarchy. The dire consequences of such lurid and quixotic prepossessions are everywhere visible, from an impoverished and totalitarian island off the coast of Florida to once-prosperous Venezuela sinking into the Ninth Circle of Hell to a collective European ally collapsing from within owing, at least in part, to the unsustainable reverie of universal peace and contentment. And it doesn't stop there. The Utopian virus seems to be spreading almost unchecked, sometimes furtively, sometimes aggressively, with predictable results.

Investing one's thoughts, feelings, energies, convictions and strategies in the effort to build a "no place" will result inescapably in establishing a "bad place," a *kakotopia*, in which only the elite can prosper. The 2009 Romanian film, *Tales from the Golden Age*, the most recent contribution to the Utopian (or rather anti-Utopian) curriculum, documents with rueful humor everyday life in the last years of the Ceausescu regime, showing just how drab and oppressive the aureate displacement of the ordinary can be for all but the new managerial aristocracy.

Such is the travesty inherent in the Utopian compulsion, which always seems to lead to a condition of reductive squalor, the proliferation of struggle sessions, and a morbid state of public resignation. One can detect the signs of a darkening social lividity in all its coagulating symptoms and material instances. Or, in More's memorable words, Utopia represents the end "of all dignity, splendor and majesty."

The Idea of Merit

The idea of merit has fallen on evil times, as has its corollary concept, objectivity. These principles have now been breached by a consortium of the ideologically minded, who resemble a gang of robbers tunneling under a bank vault. The masterminds planning and executing this operation are a class of "treasonous" intellectuals as Julian Benda defined them, primarily academics, along with members of the political left.

In the interests of creating a society based on the axioms of "social justice"—which is really socialist justice—the principles of professional merit and scientific objectivity are dismissed by our mandarin class as forms of bigotry. As the professions, the educational institution, the political arena and the scientific establishment engage in a process of diversification, accommodating claimants who trade on race and gender rather than ability and native endowment, merit is in process of being replaced by outright mediocrity.

In the university, for example, no department is safe from the "inclusion and diversity" mania that is bringing higher education into the slough of disrepute—not Law, not Medicine, not Business, not even the STEM subjects. As is, or should be, common knowledge, Literature and the Social Sciences have long succumbed to the social justice, disparate impact and feminist miasma that has clouded the atmosphere of thought, paving the way for pervasive academic decadence.

When even Classics is contaminated by race and gender issues, we know the end is nigh. In the *Notes & Comments* to the recent issue of *The New Criterion*, Roger Kimball documents the shameful degradation of this once elite, non-politicized academic study. "Classics has fallen under the spell of grievance warriors," he writes, "who have injected an obsession with race and sexual exoticism into a discipline that, until recently, was mostly innocent of such politicized deformations." Unlike the plethora of "cultural studies" programs that now command the academic landscape—Women's Studies, Black Studies, Queer Studies, Chicano Studies, Peace Studies, Fat Studies, etc.—in Classics, after all, "You actually have to know something." The challenging nature of the subject, as well as the fact that most of its representative scholars and students appear to be white males, have rendered it suspect and ripe for demolition.

Kimball cites the fate of the Classics journal *Eidolon*, now a travesty of its original purpose, which was to foreground the relevance of classics. It has fallen to the progressivist tampering of Donna Zuckerberg (the sister) whose mandate, as she declares on her Patreon site, is to make "the classics political and personal, feminist and fun." (I always found Latin and Greek, though difficult to master, plenty fun just as they were.) Zukerberg requires that "at least 70 percent of our contributors be women and 20 percent POC." White males beware! "I have no interest," she pontificates, "in providing bland and false reassurances that we only care about good ideas and good writing and not who our authors are."

For Zuckerberg, as for most of our cultural and political power brokers, "appeals to merit" are merely "white supremacist dog-whistles." *Eidolon will enlighten us all, not only shedding "new light on the works of Alcaeus, Vergil, Horace, and Cato,"* the ineffable Zuckerberg assures us in the journal Society for Classical Studies, *but also commentary on "Sports Illustrated Magazine, the conflict between Israel and Palestine, contemporary poets' responses to the sinking of the Titanic, and the hipster obsession with kale."* The entire spectrum of a once pure and arduous discipline has been thrown under the progressivist bus and reduced to triviality and partisan hype. What goes for Classics goes for the rest of the culture—a deracination of the sources of the civilized West.

Who you are, what you feel, your race, your gender, your presumptive marginal status—these attributes now constitute your primary qualifications for preference and advancement. White heterosexual males, regardless of talent, aptitude and intellectual distinction, are naturally excluded from the new imperium. Thus, in her 2008 edited volume *Gendered Innovations in Science and Engineering*, Stanford University scholar Londa Schiebinger argued that knowledge and technics had to be opened to "new perspectives, new questions, and new missions," thus opposing "codes governing language, styles of interactions, modes of dress [and] hierarchies of values and practices" inherent in the male-dominated science and engineering faculties. She had nothing to say about levels of motivation and *discipline-specific* intelligence parameters. No matter. "We need to be open to the possibility that human knowledge—what we know, what we value, what we consider important—may change dramatically as women become full partners."

That is the "mission." It does not acknowledge that the vaunted "opening" feminists like to speak of has been in place for decades. Women now outnumber men in the university by a factor of 3 to 2 and the ratio is far higher in K-12 pedagogy. Women also predominate in the medical and legal professions, with no end in sight to their burgeoning numbers.

Nor does the sacred "mission" entail the obvious, namely, that *anyone* with the intellectual wherewithal and passionate commitment to long hours and unbroken personal discipline demanded by the subject is entitled to become a "full partner." Schiebinger's efforts to erase so-called gender bias in hiring practices by "restructuring the academic work/life balance, offering parental leave, stopping the tenure clock, and the like" are precisely what militate against laborious and dedicated high achievement. The ancillary perks, compromises and forfeitures that many women and certainly feminists seem to require effectively detract from the relentless pursuit of complex scientific knowledge in the most taxing and formidable of disciplines. Rather, whoever has the smarts and is willing to commit to the gruelling lifelong schedule necessary for the advancement of top-tier science should be welcomed into the scientific community. But race, marginality and gender are, *in themselves*, utterly irrelevant.

Tomas Brage, director of the Undergraduate Program of Studies in Physics at Lund University in Sweden, has recently published an essay circulating in the scientific community titled *What Does Gender Have to Do with Physics?*, which articulates the same premises as Schiebinger's. It is an exemplary document, worth considering not only as a screen grab of the current state of affairs but as a harbinger of worse to come. Science, like Classics the last bastion of cognitive purity, is on the way out the door. Clinical and professional debasement is now the rule in order to foster a social justice agenda.

Brage is worried about horizontal and vertical segregation, the former showing that "women and men gravitate to different fields" and the latter indicating that in academia and in physics "men are promoted at the expense of women." Brage will not countenance the idea that men and women are different, that they tend to make different choices in careers and professions, and that while men and women perform equally well under the umbrella of the Bell Curve, male nerds tend to preponderate in the mathematical and scientific standard deviation territory. For Brage, this is the result of a "strongly 'Herculean' institutional character"—in other words, it's the patriarchy at work again, privileging its own, wielding the weapons of merit and objectivity to subjugate the marginal, especially women. Brage will have none of it. "Meritocracy is a myth," he avers; "the more convinced a group is that it follows meritocratic principles, the more it is affected by bias."

Consequently, the system must be changed. Institutional culture must admit "bias-awareness training, support[ ] teamwork over a 'Herculean' culture'" that favors the individual researcher or genius, create gender diversity programs, "introduce 'counter-spaces' such as conferences and networks, where minorities can become the norm," and "counteract horizontal segregation in STEM, but avoid approaches that aim to 'change the women.'" In other words, women's needs come first, the requisites of science toggle a distant second. "Changing the women" is code for making them more competitive, work-dedicated, intensely focused-on-task at personal cost, less susceptible to the claims of biology and leisure, more willing to sacrifice personal time and resist the appeal of Zuckerbergian "fun," more "Herculean," that is, more like men. This cannot be tolerated.

Brage seems blissfully unaware that, aside from unadulterated brilliance, meritocratic traits and criteria are precisely those that STEM demands if it is to prosper. He concludes: "Clearly, the subject of all physics is affected by the background of the researcher, teacher and student, and it follows that a gender perspective is needed." No, it manifestly does not follow. The individual's *practice* of physics may indeed be affected by "the background of the researcher," but *the subject of physics is not*. The laws of nature are the laws of nature and must be dealt with on their own terms. Physics is physics — nature's handmaiden, not feminism's. Mathematics is mathematics irrespective of whether you are white, black, brown, male, female or marginal. Engineering relies on the grammar of reality, not on the rhetoric of politics or the shibboleths and fashions of the day. Rocket science is, in fact, rocket science. *The only question is: how adept are you, in the light of aptitude, desire and intelligence, at mastering the discipline.*

The issue at stake is a perennial one. The Greek comic playwright Aristophanes in a late play (392 B.C.) *Assembly of Women* (*Ecclesiazusae*) humorously pilloried the female takeover of the Athenian Assembly and dominion over the wider cultural practice. Its instigator, the early feminist firebrand Praxagora, manages to persuade her beta-male husband Blepyrus of the virtues of female control and convinces the male Assembly to hand over the reins of power to their women. The results are as hilarious in context as they are predictable in the larger world, a society descending into mayhem, pagan ritual, lack of distinction and ruthless feuding for freebies, including sexual favors for unattractive hags at the expense of their more beautiful rivals — an apposite metaphor for the war between mediocrity and merit. As scholar and translator Robert Mayhew summarizes, "Misery is not abolished, it is merely redistributed."

What does gender have to do with physics? Brage, our contemporary Blepyrus advocating for his Praxagora, asks. The question is fraudulent, a category mistake at best. The question is not a question but a commutational statement, to wit: women should be programmatically advanced regardless of aptitude, strict and undeviating devotion to the particular job at hand, examination results and credentials in the field. It is rhetorical sleight of hand. Of course gender has something to do with physics, as it does with innumerable other aspects of life and work and preference—*but gender in this sense is not exclusionary.* There is always crossover, always women in fields where men tend to excel and men in fields where women reign. This is as it should be.

The same caveat applies to all the other strata of politically correct discrimination favoring race, ethnicity, caste, marginal and identity status. Claims of "oppression" should not be permitted to dilute and bypass norms of accomplishment that govern the properties and exactions of any discipline or profession, whether it be Physics, Engineering, Technology, Law, Medicine, Business and Economics, English Literature, Classics, or any other trade, craft, function or vocation one can think of. Neither from the moral, epistemological nor economic point of view can "outcomes," ideological "inclusion" or the phantom of "diversity" be legitimately compelled or manufactured. Indeed, why "diversity is our strength," as the slogan has it, has never been adequately explained. It is just as likely, as we have seen, to generate conflict and disunity, disparities of talent and motivation, the tendency to ghettoize and the weakening of common standards. That way lies societal perdition. No culture or nation can long survive collectively enforced mediocrity.

In short, all should enjoy the *opportunity* to compete and perform to prove they satisfy the conditions of a particular field of endeavor, to demonstrate excellence, merit and respect for truth and objectivity. No concessions should be made that adulterate the principles of the discipline, trade, service or profession under the loupe—unless we are willing to allow discovery and inventiveness to flag, analytical and conceptual quality to decline across the board to everyone's disadvantage, and "misery to be redistributed." Plainly, no one should be prevented from lining up at the starting gate, but the race must not be fixed. To cite the poet John Keats, that is all ye know on earth and all ye need to know.

Life in the Biodome

The Bloedel Conservatory, a triodetic biodome located in Queen Elizabeth Park at the highest point in Vancouver, Canada, houses more than 120 free-flying birds and 500 exotic plants and flowers in a temperature-controlled environment. It was financed by a lavish gift from timber industrialist Prentice Bloedel in the mid-20th Century and built by the ten Van Vliet brothers, founders of the Double V Construction Company. Donor and builders of the impressive biodome were inspired by a sense of civic duty and love for the city; however, the biodome's continued existence was by no means underwritten. It was nearly demolished when the Vancouver Park Board voted to close it due to "declining attendance and growing repair and maintenance costs," but was saved by the Friends of Bloedel Association and other groups that lobbied to preserve the heritage landmark, bolstered by a providentially sharp increase in attendance numbers.

When my wife and I visited a few months back, I was astonished by the avian proliferation, innumerable species of colorful birds—Java finches, Lavender waxbills, Senegal doves, reedings, parrots, mannikins, Guinea turacos, Napolean weavers—picking seed and twigs on the labyrinth of paths indifferent to the crowds that shuffled past. Mice scurried back and forth as if they owned the place, harmless and safe. Cockatoos orated on their soapboxes. The purling of the Saffron finch was indescribably lovely. Receptacles for food and vessels for water were constantly being re-filled by volunteer attendants; others swept the paths and removed the droppings. The air was redolent with the rich scent of exotic perfumes. Nature had been civilized.

I could not help reflecting that the biodome was in a certain sense a metaphorical surrogate for Western civilization, evolving through a long history of trial and error into a comparative haven for its cultural and national species. It provided a favorable environment for human flourishing, bestowing a degree of shelter, sustenance, leisure and freedom never before seen for those who would otherwise have found themselves in a state of nature where life, as Thomas Hobbes famously wrote in *Leviathan*, is "solitary, poor, nasty, brutish and short." The Greeks gave us the idea of the sovereign human mind and the Judeo-Christian nexus bequeathed the idea of the infinitely precious human soul. These gifts were the materials from which the biodome of the West was gradually assembled.

At the same time, it was obvious that our parabolic biodome was by no means assured and was always susceptible to dereliction from various forms of dysfunction and the inevitable factors that plague all human constructs and institutions—analogically speaking, "declining attendance and growing repair and maintenance costs." In real-world terms, the biodome of Western civilization—of the rule of law, however honored in the breach, a free market economy, the separation of church and state, a functioning infrastructure, property rights and individual autonomy—is now increasingly plagued by the ills of cultural exhaustion, historical amnesia and personal apathy. The volunteers are falling away, forgetting that, like a heritage building, the structure has to be jealously guarded and attended to if it is to survive.

Moreover, the actual biodome seemed to me the very antithesis of another and figurative biodome, a fiction of the political imagination in which life would finally become a utopia of collective equality and realized human happiness, a social and economic paradise on earth. It was aptly described in a fascinating play by Belgian playwright Michel de Ghelderode (1898-1962), titled *Christopher Columbus*, in which the protagonist draws up an imaginary map of the new world to be discovered that includes: "Strange flowers, oils, palms, gold nuggets. Gold, gold everywhere, rivers of gold, cities of gold, gold and feasting, wines, tall lascivious women! Feasting and sacrifice!...It is understood that no one ever works there. What rapture!" Unfortunately, new world votaries, Columbus laments, "have no idea of the orgies that threaten, of the sins, the dreadful sins that they will commit."

Socialists, our new world votaries, believe they are working against the inequalities of the capitalist system, forgetting about the even worse inequalities of the socialist system. What they do not understand is that socialism doesn't work because human nature is flawed; greed and envy will always emerge to corrupt any and every human endeavour, system or institution. As America's second president John Adams wrote in 1814, "Those Passions are the same in all Men under all forms of Simple Government, and when unchecked, produce the same Effects of Fraud Violence and Cruelty." Adams was accordingly pessimistic about the prospects for naked democracy—unless, of course, America abided by its 1788 ratification as a constitutional republic. In the celebrated words of Ben Franklin, "America is "A republic…if you can keep it."

In this regard, lawful capitalism, free enterprise and anti-trust oversight epitomize, for all their defects and contradictions, probably the best of all human attempts at governance, causing the least amount of individual harm and economic distortion. In principle, the best system of social and political administration is doubtlessly an enlightened despotism—one thinks of Marcus Aurelius or of Prussia's "philosopher king" Frederick the Great—but the problem here is obviously that of a guaranteed succession.

There can be no question that socialism in all its forms is a human and political disaster. The Soviet Union was a gigantic failure. Apart from the members of the Politburo and its scientific echelon, its population faced chronic food shortages, rationed goods, punishing quotas and long lineups—the infamous "empty shelves" phenomenon. Its satellites and clients did no better. No one knows how many millions succumbed in the gulags and died of forced starvation. Cambodia was hell on earth, approximately one third of its people falling to the murderous whim of the Khmer Rouge. After an estimated 70 million deaths, Maoist China had no option but to eventually install a mixed economy. Venezuela, once ranked the 4th wealthiest country in the world, now sits at 126th on the Legatum Prosperity Index and is utterly devastated, along with socialist Zimbabwe a collective basket case. Under the sway of an unelected bureaucracy, welfare state Europe faces high unemployment, declining wages, massive debt and social turmoil. The Socialist Republic of Canada is presently economically stagnant and prey to astronomical debt load, its future likely mortgaged for generations. The socialist biodome is slated for bankruptcy.

Simply stated, individual freedom and collective equality are necessarily incompatible. History has shown that the former is preferable to the latter, producing greater happiness or, any rate, less unhappiness. One might say, then, that the conflict between liberal democracy and centralized state management, between regulated competition and authoritarian technocracy, between conservatism and progressivism, between, in a word, capitalism and socialism could be described as a contest between a real biodome that requires labor and vigilance to ensure its persistence, and a fantasy biodome that exists only in theory and has collapsed everywhere it has been tried. Capitalism for all its shortcomings has found a way to work with human nature and at least to *limit* the political and systematic incursion into the arboretum of human liberty—to nourish the human spirit, to preserve the beautiful and the fragile, the siskin and the tanager, despite the inevitable social and economic disparities that ensue.

Human nature always wins, but its victory can be tempered. Western civilization is the only antidote, however partial, to the vices and depredations of our nature and it must be defended at all costs. It represents the battle against ourselves which socialism has conceded. The biodome cannot survive otherwise.

The Shemitah

I have never been partial to doomsday scenarios of any stripe. End-of-the-world prophecies have always left their proponents in the throes of revisionary confusion, manically adjusting their calculations and hoping to get it right next time, and the time after that, *ad vomitatum*. Population gurus promise mass starvation while the food supply defiantly increases. Flood experts inform us that the entire eastern seaboard will soon be under water but ocean levels remain insolently stable. Global warmists predict an atmospheric inferno while the temperature refuses to comply and the next ice age gradually but inexorably approaches. And so it goes.

Meanwhile real threats to our wellbeing and even to our existence are serenely disregarded: for example, asteroids from space, an EMP attack neutralizing the electrical grid, or the cultural debacle of unrestricted Islamic immigration and the crisis engendered by open borders. These are exigencies that can be met, given the mental alertness and political will to prepare for and defuse them.

Doomsday scripts and warnings are another matter, figments of the realm of theological speculation or pathological fantasy. Yet one must always allow for a possible exception to the general rule, if only to avoid the intellectual rigidity of epistemic and ideological dogmatism. The future, like science, is never settled.

Recently I've been reading Jonathan Cahn's two disturbing books, *The Harbinger* (a novel) and *The Mystery of the Shemitah* (a long expository essay), foretelling the imminent collapse of the United States. Cahn, who bills himself as a messianic rabbi and pastor, is a dreadful writer, repetitious to the point of reader catatonia, enamored of the trick of posing obvious rhetorical questions and then answering them as if he were pulling a rabbit—or a rabbi—out of a hat, and occasionally prone to assuming premises. To take just one example of the latter, the Christian site *Lighthouse Trails* explains that pluralistic America's relation to God is very different from God's relation to theocratic ancient Israel—the one initiated by man, the other by God—which Cahn presumes to be equivalent. And yet, for the most part, the evidence he marshals for the revelation he relentlessly advances is, on the whole and despite some misfires, rather compelling. The books need to be closely studied if one is to get the full brunt of his thesis, but his argument can be stated in cameo form, an injustice, to be sure, but necessary in a limited context.

Shemitah is the Hebrew word for "release" or "remission," referring to the Sabbath Year enjoined by the Lord in the *Tanakh* (the Hebrew canon) as an obligation upon the children of Israel. Every seventh year the nation is required to leave the land fallow and to cancel all debt and credit, a year of cessation from productive activity commemorating the seventh day of creation when the Lord rested from His labors. The *shemitah* is an acknowledgment that the land belongs not to the people but to God and that all blessings and prosperity flow ultimately from the Divine. However, when it is ignored or forgotten, the blessing it entails upon the people of Israel morphs into a judgment of disaster. This judgment is foreshadowed by nine harbingers, adumbrated in the *Book of Isaiah*—recorded as the Breach, the Terrorist, the Fallen Bricks, the Tower, the Gazit Stone, the Sycamore, the Erez Tree, the Utterance and the Prophecy—intended to warn the people to change their ways and return to the terms of communion and observance. But should the auguries fall on deaf ears and blind eyes, calamity inevitably ensues in line with a strict biblical schedule.

Cahn contends that the harbingers apply not only to ancient Israel but to contemporary America, which was founded on principles that formally established it as a second Israel and a nation consecrated to God. We have in mind the words of dedication from George Washington's first presidential address: "there is no truth more thoroughly established, than that…the propitious smiles of Heaven, can never be expected on a nation that disregards the eternal rules of order and right, which Heaven itself has ordained."

The literal conditions of observance may have changed, but the recognition of grace and benediction, the belief that the nation has been consecrated, remains binding. Should the nation turn away from its origins and betray its hallowed commitment, it will begin to break apart. "As did ancient Israel," Cahn writes, "so now America began removing God from its national life, from its culture, its government, and its public squares." Cahn's narrative surrogate in *The Harbinger* pronounces his own judgment on America: "America must now face the magnitude of its moral and spiritual descent, the degrading of its culture…and the altars covered with the blood of the innocent." For among the multitude of its sins, we come to understand, America is sacrificing its unborn in record numbers. As a result, the nine prophetic signs of judgment have now come to pass, which Cahn charts with mathematical and graphic precision, making his warnings hard to dismiss as the hallucination of yet one more cracked soothsayer. The biblical template has been followed to the letter.

Like Israel at the time of the Assyrian and Babylonian invasions, America appears set to founder, militarily, financially and economically. Although I am a skeptic by nature, I readily confess to considerable distress, for I cannot simply wish away the many strands of evidence Cahn presents. Each one by itself may be regarded as problematic, but taken in their entirety the tapestry he has woven is quite terrifying in its completeness, vividness and uniformity. In short, his accounting is unlike the fanciful prognostications of the general run of catastrophists, whose predictions always fail to be realized. Cahn is on to something and should be read with an open mind.

* * * * *

What Cahn sees as a biblical prophecy I see as a perfect storm, a levy of forces, events and developments coming to bear upon America — and the West — at approximately the same time, historically speaking, and working eerily in unison. By a strange quirk of serendipity, before I had opened Cahn's pages, I was drafting a series of notes toward an essay on the subject of America's decline, in which I had also compiled nine signs or harbingers of my own, which I called "portents" and "heralds" presaging a coming collapse. True, these auspices were not based upon a biblical pattern and they did not march in the systematic order of Cahn's harbingers, nor were they plotted on a temporal graph. But taken in their aggregate, they seemed incontestable in their collective momentum and persuasiveness. I list them in no particular order from the notes I had assembled, pre-Cahn.

Education. American K-12 education, with its inbred pedagogical and curricular decrepitude, has been further compromised by the entrenching of the Common Core program, characterized by coercive Federal intrusion, monopoly publishing and testing, elimination of pivotal American figures and historical events, a leftist disposition, and a powerful pro-Muslim bias.

Higher education is in no better shape. There can be no doubt that the university has been in free fall since the radical takeover of its mission in the festering 1960s, though its decline can be traced back to the "progressive," child-centered pedagogy of John Dewey in the early 20th century. Standards have been lowered to admit those who are unfit for the rigors of post-secondary education; the curriculum has been both diluted and politicized; the campus has become a hotbed of revolutionary sentiment and activism; debate, argument and the free exchange of ideas are no longer part of its intellectual currency as a left consensus has shut down the expression of contrary views; feminist orthodoxy has exerted a castrating effect on university teaching and policy; trigger warnings prioritize feelings over knowledge, infantilizing a student body that must be spared the slightest twitch of emotional discomfort; and the utopian ideal of "social justice"—which properly conceived is nothing other than "socialist justice," i.e., social, political and economic injustice—has snookered the pursuit of truth and the formation of inquiring minds. In the language of Jack Cashill's *Scarlet Letters*, a critique of the cult of liberal intolerance, the university has been commandeered by an "inquisitorial" and "neo-puritanical" camarilla of administrators, professors and students. In effect, *the liberal arts have ceased to exist.*

By the same token, the professional and technical disciplines have also been corrupted by the race, class and gender shibboleths and affirmative admission policies that typify the modern academy. As *The Wall Street Journal* informs us, "four in 10 U.S. college students graduate without the complex reasoning skills to manage white-collar work." The university now graduates in ever increasing volume a class of sanctimonious and indoctrinated incompetents—a recipe for social calamity.

Gender Theory. Gender has come increasingly to be regarded not as a biological fact but as a social construct, and ultimately as an expression of one's "inner feelings" (as if there were any other kind) and affect-laden sense of sexual or personal identity. A man is a woman is a trans is a tiger is a wolf—in other words, an idiosyncratic caricature of a normal human being. This absurd and self-indulgent deformation of nature—living and thinking *A Rebours* (*Against Nature*) to cite Joris-Karl Huysman's early analysis of cultural degeneracy, has produced a society—or its patrician echelon—in process of losing its bearings, unmoored from the traditional usages that served to keep it intact. The trend toward gross disfigurement and biological subversion is merely another sign of the rampaging decadence of a culture on the skids. It is not only a random group of misfits and weirdos engaged in a fringe exhibition of self-mutilation that should concern us; it is an entire culture that is mutating away from itself.

Such aberrations follow from and go hand in hand with a longstanding, aggressive and doctrinaire feminism that has infected every important social and professional institution, leading to an attack on evolutionary biology as well as to the legal and societal depriviateging and even the feminization of men, who must not only endure institutional inequities but must continually apologize for their existence—another recipe for social and cultural catastrophe.

Immigration. Open-door immigration, a consequence of programmatic multiculturalism conceived as a social good and justified by the contentless mantra of "diversity," is a surefire source of disorder, tension and sporadic episodes of violence in the social and cultural domains. Indeed, the incursion of Islam into the West is nothing less than the latest installment of the millennial campaign to subvert and conquer the liberal democracies of the developed world. The evidence is all around us and is so convincing that only the deluded and the complicit can deny or scumble or facilitate its progress. The disaster is materially compounded by the vast influx of illegal immigrants and the millions of refugee claimants swamping the U.S. and the E.U. Europe is disintegrating before our eyes, the Commonwealth nations are gradually being destabilized, and the United States now finds itself with a growing and restive Islamic community.

Add to this the unstanchable deluge of illegal migrants from Central America, abetted by the Democratic Party, swollen by chain migration laws and encouraged by the existence of so-called sanctuary cities, and we have a country losing its national character and exposing itself to mounting domestic turbulence.

Religion. The empty pews of the mainstream Christian churches and, to a lesser degree, the reformist adulteration of the Jewish communion are obvious signs of cultural desuetude and the evisceration of moral principle, betokening the decoupling of Judeo-Christian civilization from its sustaining origins. Human beings, however, cannot live without faith in some aspect of transcendence, irrespective of how tarnished, brittle or artificial. The vacuum is ineluctably filled by pretenders to the throne, whether a belief in some secular ideology, political cause, or a competing theology such as Islam qualified by emotional fervor, self-assurance and communal solidarity (what the 14th century Tunisian scholar Ibn Khaldun in his monumental book *The Muqaddimah* called *asabiyyah*, the "bond of cohesion"). One becomes a social justice warrior or a warrior for Islam or some other substitute for what has been relinquished.

The problem is that what has been lost tends to remain lost. The customary and immemorial groundwork of values and virtues that unifies a people undergoes a tectonic shift and issues in a ubiquitous sense of social anomie, defined by the French sociologist Émile Durkheim as a condition of anxiety and disequilibrium caused by the withering of standard purposes and ethical ideals. Aside from the robust evangelical community, the U.S., like Europe, is turning away from its religious foundations, with the attendant loss of civil coherence.

Replacement Ratio. When a nation ceases to reproduce itself, the prognosis for long-term survival is patently negative. Every liberal democracy, with the exception of Israel, has fallen, some dramatically, beneath the replacement ration of 2.1, including the United States (reaching an historic low in 2013, according to *Forbes*). This is a palpable sign of impending ruination that cannot be ignored.

Western cultures grow increasingly hedonistic, concentrating on pleasure and entertainment rather than living productive and reproductive lives—Iain Bamforth remarks in *A Doctor's Dictionary* how "hedonism has turned into a kind of militancy." As marriage becomes a failing social institution, and as pro-choice abortion is now virtually unlimited, it is only a matter of time before the regenerative mortgage forecloses. Immigration may partially replenish the census, but the upshot is that the liberal democracies, and especially America with its double influx, will forfeit their civilization patrimony, shrivel and decay.

Anti-Semitism. Anti-Semitism and its cognate anti-Zionism flourish in two major constituencies: the elite leftist segment of the population and the Democratic Party. Jewish organizations like J-Street and various reform rabbinical conclaves plainly work against the welfare of the Jewish state, as does the radical wing among the Democrats, featuring outright anti-Semites like Ilhan Omar, Rashida Tlaib and Alexandria Ocasio-Cortez. Senate minority leader Chuck Schumer may fairly be described as a prominent political kapo. It is fair to say that a form of institutional anti-Zionism, the modern instance and deceptive guise of age-old anti-Semitism, has taken root in the leftist strata in the U.S. Anti-Semitism is an historically validated sign that a host nation is working against its own best interests. First they come for the Jews—then they come for everyone else, to modify pastor Martin Niemöller's famous poem. The anti-Zionism pervading the American left is another indication of the country's approaching plummet.

Race. Race relations in the U.S. have markedly worsened, in some places resembling guerilla warfare as black-on-white violence proliferates and race riots are becoming an almost weekly occurrence. The racial divide is widening rather than closing and the prospect for civil upheaval metastasizes alarmingly. The irony is undeniable: the two-term election of a black president and the installation of two successive black attorneys-general, which should have signified to most doubters that America is clearly putting to rest a troubled history, has had the opposite effect—apparently by design. A great opportunity to further the work of the civil rights movement has been squandered.

The Economy. The American economy under the statist and regulatory dispensation of post-Reagan, pre-Trump administrations was plainly on the verge of implosion. Massive unemployment, the piling on of astronomical debt, the collapse of the housing market, the insensate printing of fiat money, the downgrading of the nation's credit rating, the high cost of the carbon conspiracy fostered by the false hypothesis of anthropogenic global warming, a crushing trade deficit, and the precarious status of the reserve currency all pointed to a looming and unprecedented fiscal calamity in the making. In *The Ascent of Money*, Neill Ferguson observes that the dollar "depreciated roughly 25 per cent against the currencies of its major trading partners," bad news indeed. Similarly, economist Michael Snyder points to the negative ratio of wholesale inventories to sales in the U.S., the plunge of consumer spending to multi-year lows, and the sinking of the Dow below the 200 day moving average in the last four years of the Obama administration. These were all indices of a deepening financial crisis and an imminent major recession, which only the election of Donald Trump has managed to forestall—for now. The troubling question remains as to whether the Trump ascendancy is merely an upward spike on a downward graph line.

Obama. The legacy of the Obama years continues to infect the American polis to this day and will certainly not diminish in the coming decades. Obama was both a symptom and a cause of a decadent and floundering society, ripe for the taking. Anyone who doubts that Barack Hussein Obama was is a false messiah and a cancer on the body politic, a Marxist-trained and Alinsky-inspired radical, an Islamic sympathizer, a nuclearizing agent for Iran, a congenital liar and frivolous narcissist, a contemptible dispenser of apologies for a country that has been for the most part a force for good in a maleficent world, and the worst and most dangerous president in American history by an order of magnitude—anyone who doubts this has not been paying attention.

Add to this the redistributionist tax-and-entitlement policies he put in place, effectively robbing one class of earners to subsidize those who do not pay taxes or contribute to the GNP. As former secretary of the treasury Andrew Mellon wrote in his 1924 book *Taxation: The People's Business*, "I have never viewed taxation as a means of rewarding one class of taxpayers or punishing another. If such a point of view ever controls our public policy, the traditions of freedom, justice, and equality of opportunity, which are the distinguishing characteristics of our American civilization, will have disappeared...The man who seeks to perpetuate prejudice and class hatred is doing America an ill service...[B]y arraying one class of taxpayers against another, he shows a complete misconception of those principles of equality on which the country was founded."

It is now moot whether the United States, riven by internal dissension, infiltrated by avowed enemies and millions of so-called "undocumented workers" and queue-jumpers, drowning in unpayable debt, and vulnerable to a host of hostile nations, will ever recover or reclaim its former glory, Donald Trump notwithstanding. Of course, Obama did not appear out of nowhere; the way was already long prepared for him. But Obama himself, to use Cahn's word, was the ninth harbinger.

A considerable sector of the American public is surely aware, dimly or acutely, of several, many or all of the nine signs of approaching national collapse assembled here, even though these portents are almost universally censored or deliberately misrepresented by the liberal elite, by academia and by mainstream press and TV coverage. These entities operate under the aegis of what has come to be known as political correctness, the assault upon truth, honesty and candid expression that taints and devitalizes the culture. PC serves a triple function, namely, to suppress anything that opposes orthodox opinion or is felt as unpleasant, no matter how crucial to our wellbeing, to flatter our exalted sense of ourselves, and to promote a political agenda by masking its underlying purpose. As George Orwell famously observed and history has abundantly demonstrated, the perversion of language is a tried and tested facet of totalitarian strategy, which seeks to destroy the ability of a subject population to think lucidly and to make reasoned judgments.

Political correctness is a moral atrocity and an infallible symptom of social and cultural rot, in essence, of a reluctance to confront reality and a manifestation of the unholy terror of plain honesty. It instills a fear in ordinary folk of calling things by their right names, of speaking truth, or even of telling jokes that might offend some sensitive soul or of uttering something that seems to violate yet another in a burgeoning tally of social taboos. The result is that a culture that hides from itself cannot expect to hide from its enemies. And America, probably the most litigious country on the planet, is in the grip of this mortal disease.

Consequently, as much as I hate to say this, I do not see America unanimously heeding the decisive signs of national collapse—Cahn's nine harbingers or my nine portents, different from one another but foretelling the same end game. There have been two major "shakings"—Cahn's term from Isaiah—namely, 9/11 and the market collapse of 2007/8. His foretelling of a 2015/16 *Shemitah* event never came to pass—unless, of course, the election of Donald Trump were so interpreted by the mainstream left. But I strongly suspect that a third "shaking" is in the offing.

In one of the most stunning of Cahn's correlations, he points out that Ground Zero, the locus of the first great "shaking," faces and was owned by St. Paul's Chapel, where on April 30, 1789, immediately following his inauguration in New York City, "George Washington, the nation's first president, [accompanied by] the Senate and the House of Representatives, bowed together to consecrate the new nation's future." Ground Zero was America's ground of consecration. It became the

Valley of Jezreel. According to Cahn, the Divine blessing had been transformed into a Divine judgment and the sacrament had turned into a punishment. America had been warned.

There are a number of ways, as I indicated at the outset, that I'm not in complete sympathy with Cahn. Additionally, Cahn posits the necessity for a collective rebirth of faith and the re-establishment of an original covenant, which *Lighthouse Trails* rightly emphasizes is inconceivable. Nor can I accept the Christological apologetics of Cahn's conclusion. I am not able to take Jesus into my heart, any more than I can convince myself I would have liked the patriarchs or the prophets if I would have had to live with them, rather than merely reading about their exploits and absorbing their profundities. Admiration is not conviviality and respect is not intimacy. I don't know where I stand with regard to the sacramental but I can recognize immorality, deceit and corruption when I see it, including in myself. I don't write from a holier-than-thou perspective. Nevertheless, the warning signs of a cataclysm from which we may all suffer, the fall of the once-greatest nation on earth, has left me "shaken."

The question I now pose is paramount. Can the desired election of a responsible and patriotic conservative administration, such as the one that Donald Trump is manfully struggling to bring into being, undo the damage and reverse the tide of devastation? It seems unlikely to me. America's legendary economist Thomas Sowell is equally fearful, as he told *The Washington Times* (March 5, 2019), "that, in the long run, we may not make it." Yet, as Sowell continues, "There are so many things that we can't possibly know. And so, we may make it, but I wouldn't bet on it." The key is "we may make it" because the future is unpredictable, whether we bet on it or not. Such is the only species of "hope and change" that is authentic, that is at least theoretically conceivable, and that really matters.

www.ingramcontent.com/pod-product-compliance
Lightning Source LLC
Chambersburg PA
CBHW050143170426
43197CB00011B/1939